Think BIG GER

How to raise your expectations & achieve everything

Michael Hill

with Paul Little

RANDOM HOUSE
NEW ZEALAND

With thanks to Paul Little

A RANDOM HOUSE BOOK published by Random House New Zealand
18 Poland Road, Glenfield, Auckland, New Zealand

For more information about our titles go to www.randomhouse.co.nz

A catalogue record for this book is available from the National Library of New Zealand

Random House New Zealand is part of the Random House Group
New York   London   Sydney   Auckland   Delhi   Johannesburg

First published 2010. Reprinted 2010, 2011.

© Michael Hill 2010

The moral rights of the author have been asserted

ISBN 978 1 86979 411 8

Illustrated by Michael Hill
Layout and cover design: Monika Hill
Cover photo: Mark Hill
Printed in New Zealand by Printlink

I dedicate this book to you . . .
but only if you are about to change . . .
to push harder and achieve what, to
others, might seem impossible.
Yes, I dedicate this book to you.

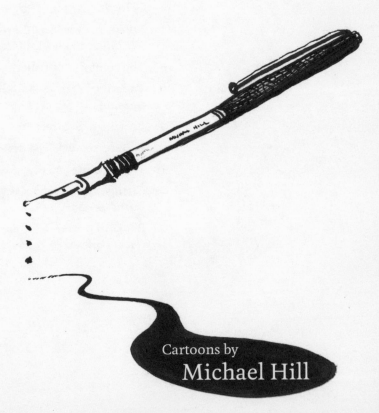

Cartoons by
Michael Hill

Contents

Before you begin

Deep down inside, do you ever get the feeling there must be a better way to live your life? That life for you is like living on a treadmill; you are in a rut and cannot see a way out, let alone any distance ahead.

I discovered a better way — some of it by accident, some by my own failures and some from misfortunes — that has taken me on a new path to places I never knew existed.

If you have bought this book but are not planning to change your life, please do not read any further, but give it to a friend who will make good use of it.

How to use this book

Still here? Good. There are just a few simple rules to help you get the most out of this book and learn to think bigger the Michael Hill way.

You will discover a different way forward and be able to look at yourself from a different perspective; see how unique you are and how much potential you really have. This will enable you to set goals, think bigger, stop worrying, be healthier and even have time to effortlessly enjoy life.

You will also discover it is not just one thing that makes the difference between success and failure, but a combination of many small things that we often overlook and, if left unattended, mar our path to our biggest potential.

The book is divided into three main sections:

Work
Life
and Balance.

And there is a final section that sums up the philosophy of Thinking Bigger the Michael Hill way.

Why work, life and balance? Because everyone talks about work-life balance, but hardly anyone does anything about it. I want to change that. It is only by understanding the relationship between work, life and balance that you can free yourself to think bigger than you ever believed possible.

You can read these sections in any order. This book is designed to be read and reread. You might like to keep it beside you at all times. On your desk. Next to the bed. In your car. You'll find it gives you solutions, challenges and inspiration when you most need them.

And be sure to practise what you find in here. Apply the rules. Test them for yourself. Don't take my word for it. The aim is to get you ready to think bigger.

Are you up to the challenge?

Work

You won't get anything unless you have the vision to imagine it.

John Lennon

the key!

1. At the goal face

The first & most important rule for thinking bigger successfully is to set a goal and contemplate where you want to go. Where do you want to be and what do you want to be doing in 30 years' time? If you've never thought about it, shut your eyes and imagine yourself three decades from now.

Let go of all the old baggage you may be carrying around; forget all the negatives that could be in your way. Forget the fear of not trusting your inner instincts. Forget your age, as how young or old you are makes no difference. Forget any weaknesses or disabilities you may have.

Now, fling yourself without any inhibitions into visualising what you want to stand for.

What do you want?
What do you
really, really want?

What are you doing in your mind's eye? What is the first thing that has popped into your head? Whatever it is, it's probably correct.

By the way, you can set goals at any age. With the right attitude to health and a few simple preventive measures — which we will talk about later in this book — you can almost certainly count on another 30 years, even if you are past what used to be called 'retirement age'. (Retirement is something you won't be hearing much about in this book. I don't believe in it.) In fact a goal will probably extend your life.

One of my heroes is Antonio Stradivari, the great violin maker. He lived in Cremona, Italy, from 1644 to 1737 — a time when the average life expectancy was 35. He survived famines and plagues that devastated the populations around him. His goal was to create a perfect violin. His instruments are masterpieces in their own right. He was always striving to make the perfect violin. No matter how good he got, he always wanted to be better.

All his measurements and drawings have been analysed by computer and been shown to be absolutely perfect, although all he had to work with were his hand and eye. At the same time, every instrument was different because of the different woods he had to use. He could sense that one piece of wood was different from the wood he used in the last violin and would almost instinctively make minuscule adjustments to allow for that. He had a drive to achieve something and didn't want to let go of life until he had achieved it.

Antonio Stradivari died at the age of 93. He had found the key: to be able to discover in yourself what it is you really would like to do and to not doubt yourself.

> **Stradivari had found the key: to be able to discover in yourself what it is you really would like to do and to not doubt yourself.**

On the other hand, there are successful people who haven't worked out a 30-year goal. I can only imagine what they will achieve when they do.

One of these is the inspiring New Zealander Kevin Biggar, who has rowed the Atlantic and walked to the South Pole among other achievements. When I met him I asked him what his long-term goal was and he said he didn't have one. He's very goal-orientated, but he didn't have that long-term vision.

But that is not unusual. Very few people think 30 years ahead. This is the key to achieving bigger things. Seeing that approximately only half a per cent of the population do think this far ahead, it gives you an enormous competitive advantage.

So, what is your vision? When you close your eyes, do you see yourself hiking in the Himalayas, working to end child poverty in your home country, collecting your BA, welcoming guests to your Michelin-starred restaurant or managing a successful Michael Hill store?

Can you imagine it? But I want you to think BIGGER.

Now, imagine yourself climbing Mt Everest, collecting a Nobel Peace Prize for ending global child poverty, collecting your PhD, opening the fifth in your chain of Michelin-starred restaurants or managing 300 stores in a foreign country for Michael Hill.

Yet if you asked anybody on the street 'What are you going to be doing in 30 years?', you'd get a shrug of the shoulders and a blank look in almost 100 per cent

> **People who have a 30-year goal will achieve bigger results** far quicker than they imagine.

of cases. Very few people know where they are going in the long term. Result: they don't achieve their full potential. People who have a 30-year goal, on the other hand, know exactly where they are going and will probably get there far quicker than they imagine.

I break it down into three phases so it's easier to handle. Every 10 years is a stepping stone for raising the bar yet again. So every 10 years your expectations and thoughts will move you closer to your long-term 30-year target.

Even Stradivari seemed to do this every 10 years of his long career. He was ripe for change every decade. Until 1690 he was still producing violins based on the excellent model of Nicolò Amati, the violin maker from whom he learnt his trade. In the next 10 years he was determined to branch away and make the perfect violin. From 1690 until 1700 he began producing a long-pattern

Don't fool yourself into believing you can achieve greatness without 100% commitment and focus.

violin that was different from any that had ever been made. From 1700, for 10 years, he abandoned his long pattern totally and tentatively made the violin into a new form that was fuller in the body with a bigger and more robust sound. By 1710, at the age of 66, he was producing his grand pattern, which was the climax of his career. He worked on and tried to improve this over every decade until he died at 93.

Stradivari proved the point back then. He is possibly the most well-known person of his era, having produced around 1500 violins from his small workshop over four decades. On today's market those violins would be worth around $4.5 billion.

To set 30 years as a starting point, to me, has great significance. It gives you time to do something substantial. Thirty is the starting point.

The key is to put a stake in the ground and make it happen. You must believe in what you are about to do and be willing to fight for the outcome. Lots of people you know who are sitting on the fence will try to encourage you not to bother. But be strong and make the moves now to alter your life forever.

I can't emphasise enough that goal setting won't work until you actually tell yourself it's going to work. The brain has to make the connection. And then . . . it's like the change that comes over someone when they've been putting off making a difficult decision, such as ending a relationship or leaving a job that is making them unhappy. When they finally make the break, the stress leaves them immediately; they look younger overnight and have a great sense of freedom.

Why bother?

Beware of words that lead us nowhere. Beware of others' negative or pessimistic comments. It is too easy to opt out of doing something because of our fear of uncertainty. Once I started out on my venture to open a chain of jewellery stores, I heard a lot of this: 'Why are you bothering? Why aren't you happy just enjoying life and having fun?' Who cares?

No goals, no outcome

I had tried very hard to enjoy just playing golf every day and being semi-retired, but it did not work for me. It was nowhere near as exciting as having a bigger goal for me and my associates to achieve greater things — which gets us back to goal setting.

If you don't have goals that are big and clear enough to see, the easy option is to settle for 'Why bother? I'm content doing what I am doing now.' But think about it! Is this really where you see yourself in 30 years? Standing still except for some limited goals that barely push the limits of your potential? The thought of just lowering my golf handicap didn't do it for me.

A lot of people don't know how to choose a goal, but once they've decided, then getting there becomes almost effortless. The rest takes care of itself. We can just about go on auto-pilot if we have set our goal and can see it quite clearly.

The goal is the catalyst for everything you want to happen. Once we have put the stake in the ground and committed ourselves to do something, then everything else in our lives feeds into it.

To see our goal — and the path to reaching it — with the most clarity, we

'I believe in myself and in the fact that our life is what we make it. If we want something very much, then this is what will happen.'

Sylwia Gruchala, world champion fencer

> ### 'If I have seen further it is by standing on the shoulders of giants.'
> Sir Isaac Newton

need to make sure the brain is not loaded with corrupt information. We will explore later in this book a way to remove unwanted self-talk and leave room for positive goal setting. Once that is done, the rest is easy.

'Easy? But you have worked so hard to do what you have done,' people say. 'Fifty Michael Hill Jeweller shops in New Zealand, nearly 150 in Australia, 30 in Canada and you have now opened in the USA.' I would never call it hard or work, it's fun. If you have such an exciting vision, then you're going to want to do anything you can to achieve it — but it's not even possible to start without that 30-year vision — so think 30.

A prestigious university once conducted a survey of its graduates, stretching back some decades, which included a question on how many had set themselves goals when they were attending the institution. I'm slightly appalled to have to report that only about three per cent of these best and brightest had done any goal setting in their youth.

But the really startling result was that those were the students who had earned more and had achieved more in their careers.

With an exciting vision, you're going to want to do anything to achieve the outcome.

Their lives had been more rounded and they had been happier as individuals.

Personal fulfilment, we sometimes need to remind ourselves, is our ultimate aim. The 30-year goal is really about finding the right way to use our talents to achieve personal fulfilment. To find this, we must be in sync with everything around us. It may not be all about wealth, praise, honour or fame.

'Money won't buy happiness'

But it could do if handled correctly.

Money is only a problem if it becomes an obsession: a greed to have more and more than anyone else just to be classed as wealthier than your friends (or should I say perceived friends).

If we have a balance between wealth, health and happiness, and control over the time we spend on all three, then the money you gain from your goal setting is a just reward.

How to choose your goal

Are you participating in your life on a day-by-day basis, or are you going to take a long-term outlook? I believe that in everybody's lifetime, at some point, opportunity does knock and you do have an option. Grab it or let it go. If you are too comfortable and cautious you will likely give it away.

In my case, as I described in my last book, *Toughen Up*, the opportunity came when I was 40 and the house I had been building for my family burnt down with all our belongings in it. That crisis shook me out of a terrible rut and 'fired' me up, ultimately to open my first shop. I had been playing life too safe.

Until the fire, I never knew what I wanted to do. I never thought I had any capability. I couldn't see myself doing much because of my education — I did very badly at school — and having not been very successful in things. I wanted to be a violinist. That was a goal I applied myself to for a year, but that hadn't worked. I was in the watch-making business and that didn't work. I was a shop assistant, but I couldn't see myself running a shop. I was dormant, working behind the counter in my uncle's jewellery shop for 23 years before I did anything.

The house fire brought me to the crossroads where I had to make a choice. I had the option of playing it safe and staying in the family business, or starting my own business in opposition to the family's. Until the fire I never felt I had to face this issue. I took the second option; it was too obvious after the fire. The goal had been there with me all along. Dormant.

Deep in your gut there will be a feeling of something that you would really like to do. Before the fire, I told myself that opening my own shops would not have been the right thing to do. I was terrified to make a move. Then, overnight, it became something I had to do. In fact, that's another good sign that you have found the right goal — once you think of it, it becomes impossible not to do it, whether you're 15 or 30 or 70.

Beware of complacency. If the going is too comfortable, it will be very hard to act when the opportunities arise.

Not everyone is lucky enough to have their house burn down when they're looking for a goal in life. And many people may be on the right path from day one. They are even luckier.

The perfect storm

It has been very interesting owning a super yacht. *VvS1* has travelled some 17,000 hours across the South Pacific in all sorts of weather. Usually conditions haven't been too bad, but on the odd occasion I have found myself in some unpleasant, wild oceans. I have been in seas that have made my boat seem like a cockle shell.

The funny thing is that the fear of the unknown is worse than the storm when it finally comes. Until you have experienced very large seas, you are not sure what to expect. But once you have been through huge waves and winds and you and the boat have handled it, tough as it may have been, you will be back in control of your feelings. The next time a storm breaks, you will know what to do, at least up to the point of your previous experience. Then you're in for another lesson.

It's about the commitment not the goal

I know some people find the idea of committing to something for 30 years difficult to comprehend. One woman came up to me after I had given a talk and expressed just that concern.

'I like what you say,' she said, 'but I'm just going through a very painful divorce. I thought my marriage was a long-term commitment but things change. My husband said he "fell out of love" with me. What if I am ten years down the road towards my goal and I fall "out of love" with it? I might change my mind.'

'What are you doing with your life now?' I asked her.

She told me she was a teacher, but I could tell it wasn't fulfilling her. No one comes to hear me talk because they think their lives are perfect.

'Why not let yourself have an adventure?' I said. 'Changing your goal isn't a failure — it's just part of getting to your ultimate goal.'

Once we have a goal, even one that's not quite right, no effort is wasted. Pursuing it at least develops discipline. It flicks a switch in our brains from 'aimless' to 'goal-orientated'. But if we don't give our brains instructions on what we want to do, nothing will happen.

Take the addicted smoker who is always going to give up — an excellent goal, by the way — tomorrow or next week, or definitely by the end of the year. That's never going to work. You have to make the commitment first. That's a non-negotiable part of thinking bigger. One hundred per cent commitment.

Of course, for smokers, or any other addicts, a 30-year goal is a very powerful tool. It will make them want to break their habit because they know they aren't going to last 30 years to fulfil it — every cigarette is 11 minutes off their life. That's another example of something that becomes easy once we get past that first stage of finding our goal.

How not to choose a goal

So many children of wealthy parents are overindulged. Is it that some of these parents want to give their kids what they never had? Or is it that they are ego driven and showing the world they can live it up big time because they are rich?

Many wealthy families have children who run wild. Everything they ever wish for is on tap. They never have to learn the thrill of taking knocks and achieving personal goals for themselves. This is always undermined by giving them more. They have little to look forward to and no goals of their own.

How many children do you know from money-rich families who have sadly ended up in drug rehabilitation clinics or killed driving the family sports car?

Parents who give their kids exactly what they want, or force them into professions of their own choosing and not their offspring's, destroy the incentive to show initiative. They raise badly adjusted adults.

Both my children have had to fend for themselves, and in our business, my daughter Emma's promotion has only come from her peers. I have had no part in it; it was up to her to prove her abilities. At times I found this very hard, but Emma is a lot tougher for the experience.

It is harder on your children if you give in and overindulge them in too much of a good thing. Unless they can take the knocks, it's going to be tough for them to succeed in a balanced life or gain any sense of personal achievement.

Concentrate instead on the spirit of openness and sharing information that is so crucial in families.

Whether you like it or not, we're all salespeople. We use the same communication skills at home as at work. Just as you focus on a colleague's positives and don't just notice them when they do something wrong, it's important to notice when your husband or wife has cooked a nice meal, not just complain about the one that's been burnt.

The more children enjoy solid family values, the more they like to behave themselves.

Delegation is also important in families for all the same reasons it's important in business: children have to get the chance to develop responsibility. If you never give them anything to do — let alone any challenges to rise to — they will never learn to achieve greatness. Young people crave responsibility. They get pride from their achievements and develop healthy self-esteem.

Climbing over and tripping up

With our long-term goal we will find the path and the way ahead will be easy, but it won't be effortless. There is a difference.

When my uncle decided not to sell me his shop, he did me a great favour. He made it easy for me to see the way ahead — I had to open my own shop. But it still took tremendous effort. My wife Christine and I put in long hours getting our shop ready to open up against a ridiculous deadline, while my uncle tried to stop me getting insurance and stock.

That was a great help, though. It just made it easier for me to develop the determination I needed to achieve my goal. Without the obstacles, I might have coasted along.

With any goal, there will be obstacles to climb over and swamps to wade through. We can't expect the 30-year goal to be a dream ride and without challenges. It might be, but the chances are we're fooling ourselves imagining that we're going to jump over things. We're going to find things we have to get around and big trenches to scramble through. It strengthens us.

I relish the obstacles because I know that I'm going to come out of the encounter doubly strong each time.

A good barometer for how you are travelling is that if you're not making any mistakes, you're too cautious, nothing is going to change. However, the worst thing that can happen is that we keep making the same mistakes. If you keep making the same mistake over and over again, then you have a problem. So learn from your mistakes.

Your mistakes

Write down what it was you did wrong and do the 10-10-10 solution:

First 10   What have I learnt from this mistake and what effect will it have on me in the next 10 hours?

Second 10   What is the worst thing that can happen to me in the next 10 months?

Third 10   What are the best things I have learnt from my mistake that will alter my life forever and make me twice as likely to achieve my 30-year goals?

So rather than dreading making any mistakes, look at them in a new light: I will learn so much and become so much stronger through working through the three 10s.

> # As a rule of thumb, if over the period of a year you have not made a mistake (and learnt from it), you haven't been pushing yourself hard enough.

As a rule of thumb, if over the period of a year you have not made a mistake (and learnt from it), you haven't been pushing yourself hard enough.

Michael Hill Jeweller chose the wrong goal when we added Michael Hill Shoes to our business. We were thinking bigger all right, but we weren't thinking smarter. We opened on two fronts and that caused a big distraction. Keep it simple and aim at one target. Never forget:

thinking bigger = thinking smarter

Stick with what you know best: Michael Hill Shoes

With Michael Hill Shoes, we learnt a lot about what *not* to do.

It seemed a good idea to open a chain of middle-market shoe shops in New Zealand, seeing we had a strong hold on the jewellery side of things.

The biggest mistake we made was by not letting the previous owner of the Christchurch shoe stores just get on with it and run them. But my New Zealand GM at the time thought he could run the shoe stores as well as the jewellery company. Christine and I were involved with the store design, and as for the advertising, I was recording TV commercials back to back for the jewellery stores and now the shoe stores. We also discovered that shoes are very seasonal; that you have to be careful what sizes you buy, what colour, what style — all of which seems to change like the wind. Here are the lessons we learnt:

10 hours   Immediate action needed as New Zealand jewellery company monthly results were sliding.

10 months   Decided to close all seven stores.

10 years   Stick with what you know and are doing best — opening jewellery stores; don't get distracted, focus on this; keep it simple so you have some time to think and see the 30-year goal.

They were hard lessons to learn but they really sank in. The good news is we were much stronger and more focused after closing the shoe stores. So how did we turn a negative into a positive?

With a much more determined and stronger focus on growing our jewellery chain. It was the start of me thinking, well, without shoe stores as a distraction, how many stores could we have (up until this stage we had only thought of Australasia). So it was the nucleus for my 1000-store vision.

One employee from the shoe stores eventually became a manager of a jewellery store. She progressed through the company and is now in the exalted position of group diamond jewellery buyer, managing the purchase and distribution of 200 million dollars' worth of diamond stock each year. Not bad for a shoe sales girl!

Another young salesman who also decided to join us as a shoe shop assistant, came over to the jewellery side once we closed the shoe chain. He became a manager of one of our stores and at one of our annual conferences, where all managers and key staff are together, we had a day of visualising our dreams. At the end of the day each delegate wrote a dream list note on a balloon and watched it float into the sky. His wish was to be the GM for Michael Hill when we opened up in the USA. After nine years, his dream has come true. He is the president of Michael Hill USA.

So all the lessons we learnt in shoes meant it wasn't a bad thing, possibly even a good thing. It made all the team that much more able to see the big picture.

My 30-year goal

My current goal of 1000 Michael Hill Jeweller stores and making Michael Hill a world-renowned brand is the biggest thinking I have ever done. But big isn't an end in itself; it needs to be a means to the ultimate goal.

My goal is audacious but it has fired up every single person in the company. Everyone knows why they are at work every day; they're all part of reaching that goal. I've never had as dedicated and excited a group of people to work with as I have at the moment — and the people I work with have always been dedicated and excited.

By setting a goal for myself, I have inadvertently set a goal for thousands of other people who work with Michael Hill the brand.

> 'I would rather fail trying to do something big than succeed at doing something small.'
>
> *Escape to the Pole*, by Kevin Biggar

So I get to have the enormous advantage of seeing the vision I dreamt of carried out by a whole team of people, rather than just on my own — which makes the vision mighty powerful.

That goal also helps us keep our eyes on what is important in the business. When we first started out as a public company, we focused more on the short-term result than a 30-year goal. But now we are focused on where we are going, not the peaks and valleys on the way there.

Finding motivation

Motivation is easy once you've focused on a goal — that's your reason to keep going. I have a friend who is killing himself slowly with tobacco. He's a successful man, but he can't give up smoking. He knows he should give up. His smoking is seriously bad. He has to get up at three or four in the morning to have a cigarette and can't go through the night without one. There is no doubt it's going to kill him.

His underlying problem is that he lacks a 30-year goal.

His mission is that he's going to enjoy life to the full and as much as he can and when it's over, it's over. He's made that commitment. I genuinely believe that if anyone's got a powerful enough goal, they're not going to want to shorten their life.

The other day I watched a documentary on television. Two divers were going to scuba-dive with enormous crocodiles living in the Okavango Delta in Botswana. There was no doubt that the venture could lead to total disaster. One of the divers said, before he entered the dark water: 'Everyone dies, but not everyone lives!'

2. Guidebooks for the necktop computer

To make our vision a reality, we are lucky to have access to the most powerful supercomputer ever created: the human brain. It weighs in at around three pounds and needs a quarter of the food we eat just to keep it running. Our necktop computer is always ready and awaits our every command to such a degree that, if you do not programme it, it will try to understand your self-talk and act on the messages it receives.

Once we have our goal in sight, we must programme our necktop computer to help us reach it, like the computerised navigation system on a boat. We start with the point where we want to end up, then work back to where we are now. Along the way are the various islands we will stop at, reefs we want to miss, ports we will enter and leave, and, we hope, fine weather and smooth seas most of the way.

Write a book

Christine has a brilliant technique for doing this. She keeps a five-year diary. You can buy these cheaply at any stationer. Hers is just like an appointment diary but the appointments in it are goals she wants to achieve or things she would like to do.

You can put anything you want to make happen in your five-year diary. The simple action of writing it down helps implant it in your brain and increases the likelihood of it happening.

> The receptive triumph over the inflexible; the yielding triumph over the rigid. Tao Te Ching

You can make an appointment to run a marathon in one year or climb a mountain in two years, win a baking competition next week or earn a million dollars in six months. Seeing it written down with a date for a deadline is inspiring.

You can extend that concept and apply it to longer-term goals. Make yourself a 10-, 20- or 30-year diary.

When I started to write them down, I found that my goals were reached before the timeframe I had set. My computer was running at full strength.

My first goal was to buy my uncle's business. Despite everything, I couldn't make that happen. Was my goal too ambitious? Should I have settled on a more modest one? No. I made myself take on a bigger goal: starting my own shop in competition with my uncle. Soon I had three shops.

Did I sit back and relax, having achieved my goal? No. I went out and found an even bigger goal: seven shops in seven years. But it only took five years to get my seven shops. And so it went on.

Now, as you know, I have the biggest goal of all: 1000 shops by 2022.

> When you **set your goal and programme your necktop computer**, you become aware of things you did not see before you set your goal.

Programming your necktop computer is much easier than programming your desktop model. You can do it anywhere. You don't need a special language. And you don't have to worry about hackers because you've got the only password and it's all locked up inside that three pounds of grey matter in your skull.

All you have to do is write it down.

When you set your goal and programme your necktop computer, things are going to happen quickly. It's as though you've created a magnet that pulls everything towards you. It can be almost freaky at times when everything seems to gravitate to you. For instance, I might need a location for a new shop in a new town and not know where to start looking. Then I will be driving around and suddenly see the perfect space for lease. I guess that without the goal, we miss seeing these opportunities.

The programming focuses our attention. Our necktop computer has a search function. We mentally key in the term we are looking for and it will filter everything else out while it goes to find it. Something we would not have noticed at any other time will leap into our view because that is what the computer is conducting a search for.

In the same way, if you only programme it with positive outcomes, it can't see negatives. It will only deliver what you tell it to deliver. You may not be able to see a positive outcome consciously, but behind the scenes your subconscious is working away to find it for you — the same way your desktop computer will conduct a system clean-up while you go on working. Trust your brain.

Buy the book

A very good book for programming your necktop computer is Dale Carnegie's classic, *How to Win Friends and Influence People*, which contains great, simple techniques to use when working with people and is summarised in the next section of this book. His book *The Art of Public Speaking* will also help anyone develop that skill.

I let Dale Carnegie programme me back in the days when things were not happening the way I wanted them to. And I still read his book once a year.

I also enjoy reading inspirational autobiographies. Warren Buffett, Ernest Shackleton, Winston Churchill and Edmund Hillary are people who thought bigger and have written books in which they share some of the lessons they have learnt.

You may find your inspiration in stories of great generals or philanthropists, scientists or sports heroes. It doesn't matter what field they excelled in, your necktop computer wants to hear about winners in any area.

Get some guidebooks

Wherever you live, you need to get out of your environment to stimulate your necktop computer with new input. Even when I worked for my uncle, I always went away to another country for at least two weeks in a year.

As well as being able to think more clearly when you are away from your usual environment you see your normal environment through new eyes when you return. Lorraine Rishworth, who worked at a radio station in Whangarei, said something profound about travel that I have always acted on: 'When you've just come back from your trip, remember you only have three days. After three days it'll all become normal again.'

Wherever you live, you need to get out of your environment to stimulate your necktop computer with new input.

She was talking about a phenomenon we have all experienced but may never have consciously registered — when you get back from a trip you see your familiar environment through new eyes. You're a Martian for a few days. Everything looks a little strange, and you may well notice areas that need improvement or appreciate again things you had started to take for granted. You look at where you live in a totally different way for a time before you sink back into the same routine.

You will almost certainly tap into some things in your subconscious that you know you should be doing. I know that every time I've been away from home, I look at the property on my return and see things I can change. This place is paradise, but after a while you stop seeing it. It's great to get away because when you come back you appreciate what's been there all the time.

My early travelling gave me a lift, particularly when it came to business, because I would usually go and look at other jewellery shops. I picked up ideas that made a huge difference to the way I was doing things in my uncle's business. It raised the bar for me.

The simple way to discover your 30-year goal

1 Go away for a couple of days by yourself, preferably when you know the weather will be good. Choose the environment where you think most clearly, whether it's a tent in the bush, a bach at the beach or simply somewhere different from home.

2 Take yourself out of communication. That means no phones and no internet.

3 Take and cook your own food if possible — outside over an open fire is best as this is a return to nature.

4 Take a long walk or swim or a run; or row, kayak, or sail if by the beach.

5 It is best if you are uninterrupted so keep to yourself. Solitude is crucial.

6 Do not be concerned about goal setting or your wish list.

7 Keep your mind free and enjoy the experience of your solitude.

8 Have a notebook and if the urge is there write down what you want to achieve in your life. If you cannot think of anything, don't labour the point; it's not important. Just be in the now.

9 If you meditate, do it twice a day for 20 minutes.

10 After you pack up but before you arrive back home, or within 24 hours of being home, simply write down whatever comes into your head when you think about what you wish for.

It may take one or two more experiences like this to get clear directions for where you are heading, but you are now on your way. Good luck!

Chuck out the old unwanted books

I had grown up programmed with a massive amount of negative self-talk. So many things had gone wrong for me. My teachers had given up on me; I spent a year trying to become a violinist and failed; then I was sent to work with my uncle where I was a disaster as a watch maker. I guess I could be forgiven for having developed a world-beating case of low self-esteem.

Most of us have some negative self-talk programmed into our brain to a greater or lesser degree.

Imagine your brain is a library of books that needs a spring clear-out of all the old and useless volumes that will implant negatives rather than positives. Chuck them out from time to time. Clear shelf space for the volumes on your 30-year exploration project.

We have to deprogramme that negative self-talk. It is very powerful so we will need to break its shackles. Meditation is a powerful tool for this and later I will talk in detail about how to use that. In my case, there had been no room for positive messages because the negatives were so overpowering and strongly programmed. One problem is that it's easier for a negative to go in than for a positive, but clearing out the negatives gives the positives room to take root and blossom. Then the 30-year goal starts to become a dominant thought.

It's like when you're playing golf and come up to the water. If you're stuck in a negative programme, you say to yourself, 'I don't want to end up in the water . . . Got to stay out of the water . . . Look out for the water . . . water . . . water . . . water.'

Where is the ball going to go?

Take your waders.

You don't write down negatives to avoid in your diary; you write down positives to achieve. However, there may be times when you need to face a negative in order to deal with it. You may need to acknowledge, for instance, that a staff member isn't right for the company and it is time for them to move on. Or that a relationship isn't working and it might be better for you both to go your own way.

Even though it was a very positive thing for me and I knew I had to do it, leaving my uncle's jewellery business was difficult — I couldn't imagine doing it. Most people say to me they can't believe I stayed in that environment, being held back, for as long as I did. And I have to agree with them.

But the fact is, I didn't know how to get out. I didn't have anything pushing me to act in my own best interests until that fire. I couldn't see the way ahead. It's terrible and crazy and even funny to look back at now. Leaving was the obvious and only choice, but for years I resisted doing it because I was programmed with so much negative self-talk.

This voice in my head kept repeating terrible messages: 'It's not for me. I can't possibly do that. I haven't got the qualities for that and these people are so great, and I'm so pathetic . . .'

Not long after I had opened my own store, I bumped into the man who owned the local menswear store and even he had some negative programming for me. 'It's all about you and your uncle now,' he said, 'but just you wait until the day when you don't take any money and don't see anything coming in — you'll find it tough.' But there never was a day like that, and I never did find it that tough.

My computer was like a library containing books that were full of incorrect information. I had to throw them out to make space for the up-to-date books that had the information I needed.

If my brain weighed three pounds, probably two and a half pounds of it were rubbish.

It's important to remember that even successful people have this negative programming and these self-doubts. The difference between them and people who don't succeed is that they identified the doubts and reprogrammed their necktop computers.

Winners identify doubts and **reprogramme their necktop computers.**

Kevin Biggar, the rower who is still looking for his 30-year-goal, is a good example of that. He tells a story of when he was preparing to row across the Atlantic. He had been training well. He was all prepared. His boat was in order.

And he didn't know it, but he was heading for a loss.

His coach said, 'Kevin, you need to make up your mind NOW if you are going to win or not. I'm happy either way, but we need to know now. What's the plan?'

'I guess I'm going to try my best and just see what happens when we get out there on the water,' said Kevin. 'You know, there are lots of things that can go wrong … we might get some bad weather, or the watermaker might break down … I mean it would be nice to win, but you can't really hang your hat on it, there are a lot of factors …'

And his coach leapt on that.

'WRONG! You've got to decide NOW! If you decide that you're going to win, it will change everything about the campaign — the way you prepare, the way you train, the equipment you buy, the funds you need, the type of person you row with, EVERYTHING!

'When you get to the start line most of the crews will just be there to take part. But there will be a handful of teams, just a handful, that have made up their minds to win, and one of them *will* win. If you don't make up your mind now you won't even be in the same race as them.' The coach sat back in his chair and regarded Kevin coolly.

'So what's it going to be? Are you taking part or are you going to win?' Kevin thought about it and said, 'Yeah, I'm going to win.'

And that's what happened. There were two other teams really gunning for Kevin and his crewmate Jamie Fitzgerald. Kevin and Jamie rowed for 40 days — 90 minutes on and 90 minutes off — won the race and beat the record by 21 hours. It was an extraordinary endurance feat.

Kevin reprogrammed his necktop computer by changing his goal — from participating to winning — and it made a massive difference. He didn't have it to start with, but he acquired it. That's the difference between those who achieve greatness and those who nearly achieve greatness but choose or prefer to take the soft option. They haven't programmed themselves to win.

We had a similar case in our company where there had been some problems getting things right in the USA. We had just 18 stores there and they were struggling. We needed to solve a few conundrums about US retailing if we were going to reach our 30-year goal.

Our CEO, Mike Parsell, needed to go up to Chicago to sort things out on the ground, but it hadn't happened. So I thought about Kevin Biggar and after a meeting I took Mike to one side.

'Mike, are we in North America just to participate or are we in here to win?'

The next thing I knew he was on his way there for three months. He is there as I write this and I know the problems will be solved because we are definitely there to win.

You can see the pattern repeated over and over in all sorts of areas. The brain believes what you tell it. Unprogrammed, it means failure and you'll achieve it. Programme it for greatness and you'll achieve that. Programme it for sitting back comfortably once you've got to a certain point and you'll achieve that. (I should add that I don't find the idea of just sitting back at all comfortable.)

So when you are at the top of a mountain, feeling total exhilaration, and the clouds part and you see another mountain just over there that's twice as high and even more beautiful, go for it. Don't delay; the journey has just begun. Because that is what always happens — there is no standing still on the highest mountain. Even Sir Edmund Hillary went and found amazing new challenges after he had managed the greatest one of all.

The day we build our dream home is the day it burns down and we have to start again.

Push ahead; the going is easier than you imagine

The young violinists who come to Queenstown to compete in the Michael Hill International Violin Competition can stand up on a stage without a qualm in front of a full concert hall, play from memory and attempt and achieve amazing feats of musicianship. At any point in their performance, things could go horribly, embarrassingly wrong. But they have programmed themselves for success.

On the other hand, when it comes to saying a few words to the audience, I have seen these same young musicians turn to jelly. They stumble and stutter and shake as they struggle to get out a coherent sentence. Why? Not because they cannot do it, but because they have negatively programmed themselves to believe that speaking in public is a daunting task.

Even Emma Hill, my daughter and the deputy chair of our company, who has been brought up to believe she can do anything, has pockets of negative programming in her necktop computer. I'll let her tell a story to illustrate that:

Our general manager from New Zealand called me and said, 'I've got this opportunity for you.'

I had to go on TV and talk on behalf of the jewellery company. This would be the first live interview I'd ever done on New Zealand breakfast TV.

I said, 'I'm not doing that. I hate live TV. I don't want to be live because there's no chance to take your words back.' Once it's out there, it's out there. During a recorded interview for TV, I'm fine because I can just say, 'Cut' and start my sentence again and I know they'll edit it. So I was pretty freaked out by having to do this.

'Why don't you do it?' I said to the GM.

'I can't,' he said. 'I don't have the Hill surname.'

I rang Michael and said, 'I don't want to do this. I hate live TV.'

'Rubbish,' he said. 'If you keep thinking like that, it's going to be *hard. You could get yourself really worked up about this and think it's going to be so hard and get yourself in a frenzy over it, but I tell you what, you're actually going to enjoy it and it's going to be easy because it's going to come naturally to you. It's easy, it's easy, it's easy. There you go, good bye.' He was right, of course. It put me in the right mind frame and the interview went well.*

One of the things I like about that story is that even after all these years and all her achievements, Emma still had that pocket of negativity. We all carry these things around with us. So it doesn't matter what stage you're at along the road to your goal or how competent you are, you can still reprogramme yourself to do better. Be aware of your fears because they're not going to disappear, but you are going to learn to deal with them.

In fact having fears is a positive because it makes you prepare properly for things. If you're not fazed by anything, then you don't put that much work into it. It's when you push through the fear barrier that you start to do interesting things.

The three-pounder

The average brain weighs about three pounds (1.4 kilograms) or two per cent of your body weight. (Albert Einstein's brain was slightly smaller than average, though it appeared to punch well above its weight, so to speak.)

Your brain produces more power than is needed to run the light in your fridge — 10-23 watts when awake.

Twenty per cent of the oxygen you consume is for your brain.

If you laid them out end to end, the blood vessels in your brain would be 160,000 kilometres long. That's enough to go around the equator four times.

The brain has 100 billion neurons. There are between 1000 and 10,000 synapses for each neuron in your brain.

If you get in an
argument make
sure you lose.

3. Books that made a difference: 1

How to Win Friends and Influence People
by Dale Carnegie

This book was first published in 1936, in an edition of just 5000 copies, and has never been out of print. Its author began researching the principles it contains years before, which means that many of its lessons have stood the test of time for nearly 100 years.

Dale Carnegie provides solutions to one of the basic human dilemmas: how to get along with and influence people in our everyday business and social contacts.

It has had a profound effect on me and on the more than 15 million other people who have bought it. A few of its main principles are outlined here, but I recommend you also buy the book and absorb the wisdom to be found on every page.

Carnegie's key insight is that people want to be respected; if you genuinely acknowledge them as human beings rather than sales prospects, you are likelier to get a good response. They will want to work with you because you make them feel good.

People will be well disposed toward you if you are genuinely interested in them. It is the good listener who gets the reputation as the good conversationalist. Instead of trying to show the other person how interesting you are, draw them out to talk about what they find interesting — they will end up thinking you are the most fascinating person they have ever met.

Carnegie says you should never get into an argument or try to prove a point in business. If you do, make sure you lose, because if you win you will leave the other person feeling so bad they will not want to have anything to do with you. Coupled with this: Don't tell people what's wrong with them, their ideas or their business; tell them what is right. Rewards are far more effective in changing behaviour than punishment.

Finally, my favourite piece of Carnegie advice — smile. First impressions really are the most important — they set a note that will be maintained throughout any relationship. And a smile is simply the best way of making a good first impression. Everyone likes happy people and they like people who are obviously pleased to see them.

4. Believing is seeing

Having cleared our brain of negative self-talk, we are ready to bring in the big guns and aim them at our goal. One of the best known and most powerful of these weapons is visualisation.

You would expect the world's greatest golfer to have the world's greatest caddy by his side, and few would argue that Steve Williams, who caddies for Tiger Woods and has also worked with the likes of Greg Norman, Raymond Floyd and Sir Bob Charles, is just that.

Hitting the Zone: Golf at the Top with Steve Williams, by Steve and Hugh De Lacy, is a brilliant account of the mental side of the game and full of advice on how to harness the power of the mind to think bigger and give you the winning edge. I have had the pleasure of meeting Steve Williams and find his book an inspiration, not just when playing a round but in many other areas as well.

His chapter on visualisation — how to get what you want by creating a picture of it in your mind first — is one of the best accounts of that practice I have ever read. Visualisation is a crucial step in the process of seeing and attaining our goals. It is also one of the easiest mental exercises to perform because we all have an imagination.

Some people say that dreams in the ancient stories of great heroes, such as Agamemnon dreaming of victory before a battle in

> **Visualisation is a crucial step in the process of seeing and attaining our goals.**

the Trojan War, were really descriptions of visualisation. Did the famous oracles, such as those at Delphi in Greece, who seemed able to predict the outcome of important events, actually visualise the result and communicate that to those who came to seek their advice? The ancients almost certainly used some form of visualisation, as so many of their legends tell of visions of things that came true.

Unlike your desktop computer, the necktop computer can use its imagination to create images that don't exist — in other words, to visualise results that don't exist yet, but that you want to have come true in the real world. Computers are growing in power so quickly that soon they may be able to out-calculate and out-remember humans. But no one seriously thinks a computer will be able to out-imagine a human.

> **The necktop computer can use its imagination to create images that don't exist yet . . . but that you want to have come true.**

A golfer can use his imagination to see the perfect shot happening before he hits the ball. He can incorporate the hole he is playing — the landscape right there in front of him — and overlay it with a 'mental movie' of the perfect shot. Steve Williams writes: *We need to employ the imagination like a video or movie camera to demonstrate to the subconscious, in perfect detail and vivid colour, exactly what the perfect golf shot looks like every time we address the ball.*

The saying 'A picture is worth a thousand words' could not be more apt than when applied to the imagination's capacity to influence the subconscious in real time. Affirmations take a month to fully penetrate the subconscious. Visualisation — the imagination — penetrates immediately.

According to Steve, the golfer starts to focus on the ball as he approaches it. He visualises that ball being hit, going up into the air, seeing it hit the ground, bounce and even where it will end up. If the golfer can empty his mind of all self-talk and distractions and have no thoughts in it except that vision he has programmed into his necktop computer, then when he hits the ball his brain will do the work and give him a hole in one on every par three.

You can make your visualisation even stronger by using all your senses — imagining not just the sight but the sound of the club hitting the ball perfectly, the smell of the grass and the air, the touch of your hand on the club and the breeze on your face, and the taste of the air in your mouth. (You might imagine the taste of victory, too — but that's not quite the same thing.)

Fill in as much of the picture as you can to make your vision as close to the real situation as possible. Steve suggests you think of all the positive sense impressions you can — your favourite sounds and smell, for instance — and associate them with your imagined perfect shot. By doing this we fill up our

> The goal seen becomes the goal believed becomes the goal achieved.

subconscious with positive impressions. Any negative concerns can't find room to take root.

Want to increase the power of your visualisation? Think bigger and see yourself executing the perfect swing.

'Take dead aim'

Why do we make things so complicated? I fumble in the semi-dark to put a CD in the disc player and try to find 'open'. I hit all sorts of buttons that look the same. Why isn't the open/close button bigger or a different colour to the others?

I like my iPhone; it's a great way to clear my emails and make

> **'Take dead aim.' Once you address the ball, hitting it has to be the most important thing in your life at that moment. Shut out all thoughts other than picking out a target and taking dead aim at it.** Harvey Penick

calls. I have to be careful, however, not to get sucked into becoming its slave as it has so many options that I could spend all day on it and forget I had a life to live. Even my car seems to have enough computing capacity to take me to the moon. To alter the clock or radio settings, or even open the fuel cap, is a mission. What a pity I can't just get in it and drive it without a master's degree in computer engineering!

As Harvey Penick said in his *Little Red Book* on the lessons and teaching acquired from a lifetime in golf: 'Take dead aim.' Once you address the ball, hitting it has to be the most important thing in your life at that moment. Shut out all thoughts other than picking out a target and taking dead aim at it.

I hear that Warren Buffett, famously successful investor, drives an older-model car that has no fancy gadgets and only uses his computer at home to play chess — sounds pretty simple.

Another great thing about the technique of visualisation is that it can be done anywhere. Of course, you want to do it just before you take that shot or go into that important meeting, but you can start to plant the messages in your subconscious long before. Ideally, you will do it when you can sit quietly with your eyes closed, but even playing it like a movie in your head when walking down the street, exercising or going to work will have a positive result.

I used to close my eyes and bring an image of seven shops into my mind when that was my goal. Now I can see 1000 shops.

We can also make our visualisation more effective by applying the Pareto Principle, otherwise known as the 80/20 rule. In this case we need to get rid of the 80 per cent of our necktop computer contents that we don't need and concentrate on the important 20 per cent.

People who boast about 'working every hour God gives' or 'always firing on all cylinders' can't enjoy the benefits of visualisation. For it to work, you need to be able to step aside and not be preoccupied by irrelevancies as such people always are.

And it works for anything. You can be pretty sure Neil Armstrong didn't visualise himself getting halfway to the moon, or Sir Francis Drake imagine himself defeating half the Armada. Whether it's a big thing or a little thing — asking that girl out and her saying yes, or selling the engagement ring, or convincing an employer to give you a job, or making the perfect sandwich — it doesn't matter what it is; if you can see it in your mind's eye, you can make it happen.

How I learnt to putt

I went to Augusta with Sir Bob Charles. Knowing he was reputed to be the world's best putter and I was the worst, I asked him what the secret was. I expected him to say I was gripping the putter wrong, or that my head was not over the ball, or I was looking up. It was none of these things!

He said, 'Get behind the ball and visualise the path it takes to the hole. See it rolling and hear it drop in.'

'Is that it?' I said.

'Yes,' he said. 'But if you don't trust your judgement it never goes in.'

Note: Although they may look similar, meditation (see page 173) and visualisation are two very different but complementary practices. One empties the mind to enable clear thinking. The other fills the mind with a clear image of your goal.

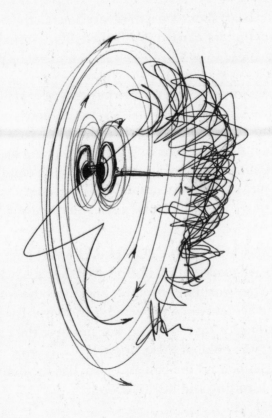

5. Books that made a difference: 2

The Three-Minute Meditator
by David Harp and Nina Smiley

One of the best guides ever written to decluttering the mind is David Harp and Nina Smiley's *The Three-Minute Meditator*. The simple meditation techniques it teaches will unlock your potential by allowing you to jettison negative self-talk and the confusing messages your brain acts on in default mode.

How to watch a movie

Harp and Smiley point out that when we watch a movie we can do it in two ways: we can become totally involved in what's on the screen so that is our whole reality; or we can take a wider view and be aware of what is going on around us in the theatre, how comfortable our seats are, how good the special effects are, etc.

In the second case, we are aware of ourselves in the situation. How does the movie make us feel? If we are with a friend, what are they are thinking about the movie? You can also toggle back and forth between the two types of movie watching.

We can do the same two things with our minds. Most of the time, we treat our thoughts as though they are the whole reality. But we can also stand back a little and watch ourselves watching our thoughts — then we realise the thoughts are not the whole reality at all. They are no more 'us' than anything we see or hear is 'us'.

This brings up a crucial idea for decluttering our negative thoughts, 'relating to our mind instead of from it'. And that means we can choose what action to take rather than just responding automatically.

Sometimes, what's in our mind when we look at it in this way will be disconcerting. We often have stressful, tiring or otherwise regrettable thoughts. So does everyone else. You can only know exactly what is going on in your own mind, but it is helpful to remember that other people are in the same mental boat. Nina Smiley says this is a case of 'comparing their "outsides" with our "insides"'.

Visualisation *The Three-Minute Meditation* way:

Who's for a slice of lemon?

This is an incredibly powerful and simple exercise to demonstrate how visualising something can make it real:

Imagine a perfect yellow lemon.

Now imagine cutting it — some juice sprays up and hits your face.

The scent of lemon fills your nose.

Now make a perfect slice, watching the moisture ooze from the membranes.

Now imagine putting that slice in your mouth and sucking on it . . .

By now, even reading this, you should be salivating.

Visualising the process has stimulated your saliva glands to produce saliva, just as it would if you were sucking on a real lemon.

This is why people think visualisation can help with illness — why can't it stimulate other glands to do their jobs or your immune system to build itself back to strength?

Visualising your future success will stimulate your senses and draw you towards your 30-year goal.

Living in the now

We spend much of our mental lives in the past or the future and too little in the NOW. Our minds are filled up with thoughts about what we should have done back then, or what we should do in the future. These thoughts can be very upsetting — lots of regrets looking back, lots of fears looking forward. As Harp and Smiley sum it up, the taste of food you are eating now is very different from a mouthful you just ate or the next mouthful you will eat.

When we are talking to someone, we often aren't in the now — we are trying to decide what to say next. We are not listening properly to them in the now, so our response is not a thoughtful, meaningful one and true communication cannot occur.

Two mind clearers

For some practice living in the now, try these two simple exercises from *The Three-Minute Meditator*:

Walking Now: Concentrate on your feet with every step. How do they feel when they touch the ground? Is the surface soft or hard? Which muscles can you feel working? Put as much of your thinking as you can into the act of walking.

Breathing Now: Concentrate on your breathing and how that feels. Is it more in your chest or your stomach? Are your breaths deep or shallow, fast or slow? Note as much as you can about the act of breathing while you are doing it. Other thoughts will be shifted to one side.

Any activity can be a Living in the Now meditation — all we have to do is become aware of it, focus on it and note everything we can about it. In doing so, we remove all our normal rapid-fire thoughts and mental clutter.

6. The comfortable fisherman

Fishing & running a jewellery store have a lot in common. If you go fishing at the bottom of the sparsely populated Stewart Island, New Zealand, it is still possible to go out with a heavy green line, three hooks and any old bait, and pull up three big cod at a time, all day.

If you do the same thing in Australia using a better bait, you might pull up two fish an hour. If you go fishing in Chicago, with an invisible nylon line and the sharpest hooks and freshest bait possible, you might catch only one fish all day. That has made the people who go fishing in Chicago tougher.

In New Zealand we are very fortunate indeed. We live in a country of endless options and huge opportunities compared to most overpopulated regions. But the problem with being too comfortable is that we find it hard to motivate ourselves to try harder. Why bother when I can catch as many fish as I like all day long?

Complacency stifles initiative. I had this problem before the house fire. I told myself everything was fine. It was, but I was too safe to want to achieve bigger things. It's easy to be too comfortable. It's much more exciting to think bigger. But it is going to take a big push to move yourself out of your rut if it is all too cosy.

> It's easy to be too comfortable. **It's much more exciting to think bigger.**

The world's best fishing

New Zealand's isolation makes it an ideal platform for experimentation. And the population of only 4 million is just the right size to trial your ideas, so you can make your mistakes and learn how to make things right before going out to the rest of the world.

If you can't make a living out of the fishing here, where the waters are teeming with fish and there aren't very many fishermen, you aren't going to make it in the waters of heavily populated and overfished countries with plenty of experienced anglers.

New Zealand is a great laboratory.

7. The winner's edge –
finding the missing five per cent

A lot of people can achieve 95 per cent of their goals. I'm interested in 95 per cent, but I am more fascinated by what makes the difference represented by that last elusive five per cent. One of the main aims of this book is to show you how to make that giant leap from 95 to 100 per cent.

The first thing we need to acknowledge is that luck has little to do with it and application has everything to do with it.

Over the years, Christine has taught many drawing classes that cover the use of and the power of observation, line, shade and how to use graphite and pencils, among many other things. The students are envious of her ability but she reminds them it has taken her a lifetime to acquire these skills. You cannot learn to draw in a few hours. You can learn the technique, but unless you keep on drawing when you are not in class, you will never improve.

The same goes for mastering any skill — learning a language, a new sport or the art of selling. You need constant practice, constant application and a lifetime of learning.

10,000 hours to success

Music is an area where people believe that talent is God-given and anyone with talent can, after a bit of practice, make it. But Professor Anders Ericsson did research that showed it takes more than a bit of practice — it takes 10,000 hours. His research was repeated by others and the figure of 10,000 hours is now widely accepted as being the minimum time it takes to become good at something.

Unfortunately, you need other qualities as well — talent, people skills, goals, presence — all the things we will be talking about in this book, but the 10,000-hour rule does remind us that practice

10,000 hours is now widely accepted as being the minimum time it takes to become good at something.

really does make perfect.

Mozart is a case in point. Certainly he was a prodigiously gifted child, who began writing concertos when he was 11, but he didn't create his greatest works before he reached adulthood. He spent a lot of time writing music and, although it was remarkable as the work of a child, it was by no means his best. A lot of it was more or less influenced by the styles of the time. But after 10,000 hours he started to really hit his straps and his genius became obvious.

This notion was popularised by Malcolm Gladwell in his study of success, *Outliers*. He interviewed Bill Gates, widely believed to be as much of a prodigy in the field of computing as Mozart was in music. But Gates spent thousands of hours working with computers before starting Microsoft. As a teenager he would sneak out of the house at night and go to a nearby facility where he practised programming on a computer that wasn't being used in those hours.

Unfortunately people took this to mean that if you spent 10,000 hours on something you would become an expert at it. What it actually means is that even the extremely talented people need that long to develop their talent to its potential.

Interestingly, 10,000 hours is approximately five years of 40-hour weeks with two weeks' annual holiday. And five years is the length of time usually required to complete a postgraduate degree or to begin to understand our business, Michael Hill.

Lead from the front

Alas, like any job, whether you have a degree or not, it still requires 10,000 hours to know the Michael Hill selling and management system backwards to leapfrog up the ranks. Ours is a different type of university. Working the shop floor and understanding our clients and how to coach and grow a team to become good enough to compete on the world stage is what our staff learn. A degree should discipline, but reading manuals is not as powerful a way to acquire a skill as the actual doing of it. It would be like getting a degree in golf by only hitting balls on the driving range compared with playing challenging courses under pressure to make the cut.

In our company everyone in management has spent thousands of hours on the shop floor selling jewellery. They have to. That is our business. Eventually things become second nature and the automatic pilot gets switched on.

At that point, they have an instinctive understanding of the business that will give them the skill set to tackle the bigger challenges that will come as they get higher in the company. Without that intrinsic knowledge from putting in the time at the bottom, they would probably fall over and not be able to get back up.

Keep learning

Working against this crucial emphasis on putting in the groundwork is the modern generation's tendency to want everything now. A lot of the people that want to work for us don't want to start at the base. You can't learn to play golf by suddenly being on one of the professional tours; you learn at the bottom, not the top.

Having a degree doesn't contribute even half a per cent to the winning edge, yet I get young people all the time who think the fact they have worked hard to get their degree means that once they have graduated they can take it easy. That was the extent of their goal setting and it spanned just five years instead of 30.

It is such a waste. They are such talented people. But they haven't yet realised you can't just study something to become good at it, whether it's medicine or understanding retail the Michael Hill way. Our people do a minimum three months of study when they join the company, but it's always complemented by real-life

Winners keep learning.

practice. You have to get out and do it — whether it's on the shop floor or in front of an orchestra. You can learn about selling from a book. But you can't learn how to sell from a book alone. It needs practice.

Be persistent

People job jump now. They don't stick to something long enough to gain the winning edge. Winners stick to things. If you chop and change every time you encounter a difficulty, you never get anywhere. I try to remind people that difficulties actually make life easier because they highlight the areas where people need to concentrate their energy.

The artist's eye

An eye and an appetite for design and detail also make a big dent in that missing five per cent.

Being artistic is a good trait to have in business and I'm very thankful to have been born with an artist's eye, which I inherited from my father. It's a gift that can't be wholly acquired. It enables you to see the difference between good and great, which provides an enormous advantage in business and gives Michael Hill the brand an edge over our competitors.

Most jewellery chains around the world seem unartistic in their approach to retailing. It shows in the shop design, the lighting, the stock and in particular the loud and inappropriate store signage.

Maintaining our artistic edge will make all the difference as Michael Hill Jeweller becomes more established as an international brand. The challenge is to make sure our store staff are disciplined as the ambience can easily be lost by staff shortcutting or thinking they know better.

I gravitate to artistic people, which is probably what attracted me to Christine, who was a secondary school art teacher when I met her. My son Mark and his wife Monika are both incredibly artistic. I am fortunate to be surrounded by an artistic family.

If you look at the great brands of the world that are associated with a name — like Ralph Lauren, Louis Vuitton, Gucci and Prada — they were built by families with a flair for artistic interpretation.

> Little differences — sometimes five per cent — make the tipping point between success or failure.

An artistic eye can be the tipping point between success or failure. There's that slight tweak, a little push, not much, and you're home. You may make that five per cent with half the effort you thought you would need.

Drive in reverse

Sometimes hard work gets in the way of success. It's all very well keeping your head down and concentrating on the job in hand, but people need to look up from their work occasionally and notice what's around them. You need to see your work space with a fresh eye.

All of us should do everything back to front on one day. Rather than going to work the way we normally do, we should go the other way around. It's important to look at life in different ways.

We practise this principle in our shops. Retail managers like hiding away out the back, working on the computer or overseeing orders. Our shops are designed with very little space out the back. It's an uncomfortable place to be for any length of time.

Instead our managers are trained to be out in the shop — and not just behind the counter but as often as not on the customer side. He or she is like a conductor and the rest of the team is the orchestra. Orchestra conductors are out the front so everyone can see them, and it's the same with our managers. They see everything from the customer's point of view. Like a lot of the ideas in this book, it's unusual, but once you hear it, it's obviously the most sensible approach to a problem.

From the front, the manager can watch and orchestrate the salespeople. He can assess a customer and make sure they are approached correctly. He can make sure that a sale is happening, not just a loose presentation. He can't do any of that if he's hidden away out the back.

It's very easy to lose a potential sale if the presentation is not done properly, especially for a pricey item like a diamond ring. There is nothing casual about it. You can't just wave a tray of diamond rings under a person's nose and expect them to make a large purchase on the spot.

It's being on top of that that makes a difference to a store's success. Anyone who can count can look after the books and sign off the orders. That's not a manager's job at Michael Hill.

Variety shows

Another principle people can lose sight of with the 10,000-hour rule is that there is more to success than just maximising your talent. Mozart, for instance, was exposed to all sorts of influences. His family was highly musical and his society was a highly cultured one, so it was the interweaving of all the influences that created the genius.

> It's important to look at life in different ways. **Broaden your outlook.**

If your focus is narrow it ceases to be concentration and turns into monomania. You are actually thinking smaller, not bigger, at that level. Broaden your outlook. By looking at the target objectively, we are able to see it from a long way off, and as we get closer, the bullseye becomes the centre of our focus.

Little things mean a lot

When you go into a cafe and order a long black or a flat white, you probably don't think very much about the process that starts when you place your order. But getting that coffee into your cup is a very complicated affair.

I have a whole book in my study on how to make coffee. It's an incredibly technical volume. It has complicated diagrams showing how the water moves through the coffee, precise instructions on how the coffee should be packed to go into the machine and much, much more. It contains everything you need to know to make the perfect cup of coffee, but you have to put all the information into practice to perfect the art of coffee making. Any endeavour we undertake has a thousand variables that can be adjusted to achieve success or failure.

> 'I don't care if you have checked it, check it again.'
> Peter Blake

These rules apply at every level. When Team New Zealand won the America's Cup it wasn't because of one big thing they did, it was because of all the little things. When you get the little things in sync everything goes right.

The more we can refine and perfect the minute details of any process, the closer we get to closing that five per cent gap and gaining that winning edge.

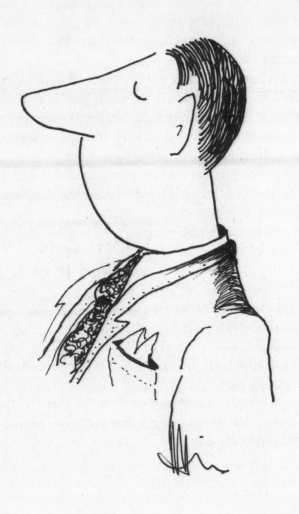

8. Present and correct

Presentation can make all the difference between success or failure. This is equally true of diamond rings, golf courses and politicians.

The way we dress says as much about us as the way we speak, stand or smell. In fact, it can send an even clearer message because people judge us on our clothes before they get anywhere near us. In order to fulfil the think bigger promise, we need to do ourselves the favour of always dressing as well as we can whether at work, on the golf course or relaxing on holiday.

When buying clothes it is best to take your partner or a trusted friend along. It is hard to see yourself as others see you, but they will see you as you really are so will offer the best advice.

Tired clothes look awful in the corporate world. Many men wear boring, ill-fitting suits and shoes, or trousers that have become shiny from being drycleaned too often, out-of-fashion ties, shirts with ill-fitting collars, ill-looking shoes with turned-up toes or too-heavy soles, or old, ill-fitting, worn belts.

In retailing today smart appearance is paramount. We are casting a critical eye over our salespeople and making sure they are dressed to achieve maximum results. The difference between being approached by an immaculately dressed salesperson and one who is less than first rate in appearance can make a huge difference to the success of the sale.

The same goes for every walk of life. But remember to dress in context: a suit on a farmer would be as stupid as gumboots on our jewellery salespeople.

I firmly believe that having natural fibres close to your skin is very good for you, whether plant-based fabrics or animal by-products such as wool. These are the healthiest material for us to wear. You feel better and they breathe, whereas synthetics have an adverse effect on your well-being.

I once had a long conversation with a senior politician, a man who has been near the country's leadership for many years. He is impressive — good-looking, informed, bursting with ideas. I was enjoying this stimulating exchange until I noticed his ill-fitting, drab suit and his feet, which were enclosed in a pair of thick rubber-soled shoes, such as you might have expected to find on a 1950s schoolboy. All his pretensions to sophistication, finesse and, most importantly, ability were undone in an instant by his badly chosen footwear and ill-fitting suit and the impression they created. These or any other minor details, no matter how small, left unattended have the potential to derail a successful politician's bid for grandeur.

So the key is to leave no stone unturned — think bigger by looking at all the small details, and get the best possible advice on all the little things that will make the winning difference. Seek expert advice on haircut, how to dress for your body shape, colours to wear for your skin and hair colour, shoes, nails, eyebrows, facial hair, perfume, breath, teeth and voice. This is the total image you portray. Make the most of yourself now.

Make the most of yourself now.

Think like a president

Barack Obama's unstoppable progress to the White House has been credited in no small part to the intensive training he received in all aspects of presentation. One of the most innovative techniques used in his coaching was silent viewing. Obama's speeches were recorded and played back with the sound off. This allowed him to assess how effective his body language, gestures, expressions and stance were and work to improve weaker areas.

Some experts in the field believe this is another example of the 80/20 rule. What people see is 80 per cent of a speech's effectiveness. What they hear and absorb intellectually fills up the other 20 per cent. Whatever the exact percentages are, there is no doubt that if one makes a poor visual impression, whether speaking to a group or to a customer across a display case, you can undermine any amount of good information or persuasive talk.

In the case of jewellery, in particular, this rule applies equally to inanimate objects, and I am often surprised at how staff fail to see the very items they are selling.

The rings are a good example of what can go wrong — and right. They are kept in a cabinet in trays according to a certain prescribed layout. At night, the jewellery is kept in a safe, and in the morning the trays are taken out to be put on display and arranged to the determined layout. If an item is sold, the rest have to be moved around so everything is still presented in the best possible way.

It doesn't look very difficult, but it is precise. When the ring is in the pad, for instance, it needs to be sitting precisely, straight upright, half out of the pad and looking faultlessly clean.

You would be surprised how many times the diamond is over on one side or facing backwards so you can't see it well, or if you can see it, there is a big finger mark on it because it hasn't been cleaned before being put back after the customer has looked at it, or the sides are dull, or the ticket that is attached to the ring is poking out from the ring slot. And then there are ring display tickets that are larger than the piece of jewellery. What would you think if you were looking at a dress in a shop or a car in a car yard and the ticket was three times the size of the dress or the car?

The basics need to be exact — a faultless presentation of each diamond ring in its display. Like the politician, a diamond ring will not be going anywhere if it is unkempt. It will end up tarnished, scratched, with a worn and dirty sales ticket and eventually be broken up or dramatically discounted to clear.

So, look at the little things and the big things will look after themselves.

You need distance to judge presentation; step back and see the small things that make the winning difference.

It's a similar situation at The Hills, my golf course in the South Island of New Zealand. Because the greenkeepers think of their job as being to take care of the course — which it is — they filter out anything else that might be worth attention, even if it is not strictly their responsibility. If they get into grass-cutting mode, the grass is in great shape, but they can't see that a tree isn't getting watered, there is a hole in the road or a leak in the watering system is not being attended to.

You need distance to judge presentation. Sometimes the staff are too close to the diamonds. They need to turn off the sound or at least stand back and check out the shoes.

So to see the trees in the forest, to see the diamond rings in the store, to see the clothes on the man . . . step back and start developing your senses to perceive the small things that will make all the difference.

The presentation of a winner

One of my ambitions is to pass on my knowledge to the winners of the Michael Hill International Violin Competition.

To reach the top in any career is a challenge and becoming a successful concert violinist is particularly difficult. Only a small handful will make the big time.

Gifted violinists usually end up studying at the great music schools of the world, such as the Menuhin (Surrey), Curtis (Philadelphia) or Juilliard (New York). They are trained in technique, musical interpretation and theory, but little attention is paid to their health, physical fitness, appearance, stage presence, dress or voice. At the MHI Violin Competition our aim is to treat each winner as a brand.

So what's the difference?

I spoke to Feng Ning, the gifted winner of our 2005 competition, on how he felt about his career. He said he was doing fine, having given around 60 concerts in the year and gradually getting his name out there. Although he is nearly there, he is still short of the mark, even if I personally class him as one of the best violinists of our time. So what's going to be the tipping point for him to become famous?

His violin is not great and, as he says, 'I'm not good-looking. If I was a pretty young girl, it would make all the difference.' I think it's more than this, so let's look at my branding method, which we are working on with our 2009 winner Josef Spacek, a 23-year-old Czech who started at four and has been playing for more than 18 years.

As our latest winner, Josef received the following critique to fine-tune his presentation to help him leap ahead with his career.

1 **Body checkout (chiropractor and physio)** and workout programme to strengthen the body. Stretching exercises. Many violinists have neck and shoulder problems because of the unnatural stance.
2 **Blood tests:** check out any possible future problems and provide supplements if required.
3 **Stage presence:** Winners have a session with a theatrical producer and are given tips to ensure their on-stage presence is spellbinding. André Rieu is the master of this — a very average violinist with an exceptional and stunning presence.
4 **Dress:** what you wear makes all the difference; we ensure our winners are immaculately presented by providing them with handmade clothing and shoes.
5 **Jewellery and watch by Michael Hill.**
6 **Hair:** cut and styled.
7 **Voice:** diction, tone.

The great music conservatories teach their students little, if any, of this. Music and perfection of technique are paramount. Yet the best technical musician in the world will not reach the top with skill alone. So I aim to give our winners a glimpse of what it takes to be a world-beater.

We apply the same criteria to Michael Hill the brand, and our people are groomed in the same way. We cannot afford to risk being in the basket of 50 maybes; we need the handful that is sure to make it.

9. Dictators and delegators

There are two kinds of bosses: dictators and delegators. I wouldn't know how to be a dictator. Every success I have had has been the result of delegating.

The dictator

I once had an incredibly talented salesman working for me. He definitely had the gift of the gab. If he saw someone looking at engagement rings in the opposition shop across the road, he would go over and talk them into coming to look at our shop and usually managed to make a sale.

He was scarily good and I made him manager of one of our top stores. It was a disaster because he couldn't delegate.

His staff were good workers but he didn't share anything with them. He took the bookwork home with him and wouldn't show anyone. The sales started to go down. In fact the store went right down to $225,000 in turnover. So he had to go. We put Mike Parsell in charge. Mike is so good at delegating that he is now our CEO. He got stuck in, inspired the staff by sharing responsibility with them and in three years that store was turning over $3.5 million.

The talented salesman's weakness, as seems to be that of most dictatorial management, was lack of trust. The question I am most asked at conferences I speak at and by people who first meet me is 'How can you find people that you can trust? I have never been able to do that.' Well I can tell you they are out there, all right, as many as you care to see. I guess you have to have faith in people's ability. See their potential and, after training them up, let them run with the job. By acting as a guide, a mentor, I have rarely been proven wrong.

The key is to not undermine them by stepping in and doing some of the job. Give them responsibility and they rise to the occasion.

In my business of 250 jewellery stores, we cannot afford to have mini dictators: those who feel insecure and feel that if they employ a better person than themselves the position they hold will be in jeopardy. They also seem to have a knack of getting the staff to assist them in choosing all replacement staff to a lower level than themselves, so the whole team ends up even weaker.

This style of management does not last at Michael Hill as all our stores' profits and losses are shown to all. Badly performing salespeople are labelled red dotters; red dotters seldom make target or additional profit.

I had another employee at a senior level who was brilliant in his special field but incapable of letting anyone else in on the secrets. The people around him were stifled and couldn't do their jobs properly. Eventually he left and we discovered he had complicated everything, including the computer systems which were purposely difficult so other people couldn't work anything out as well as he could. He moved on, we changed the computer system, let our team run with the ball, and the department is functioning brilliantly.

Dictatorship is an old-fashioned way of running a business — ruling by fear or ignorance.

I was involved in a big project not so long ago, working with a company that was run as a dictatorship, and it was quite interesting to watch.

When things went wrong, people tried to cover them up because they feared reprisals. If there was a problem with part of the job, they blamed each other. It's predictable really — if you treat people like children, they act like children.

And when their boss was away they played hookey — they went into town and took long lunch hours and came back late. They weren't doing the work they were supposed to be doing, and what work they did took 10 times longer than it should have because they were only used to working when the boss was there yelling at them.

A dictator will never have any staff who are 100 per cent committed, because people who are driven by fear don't share a goal and won't be passionate about their work. They're like the crew of a galley, rowing hard because there is a whip cracking over their heads but their hearts are not in it. If the ship starts to sink and they've got a chance, they'll leap off it rather than trying to plug the hole.

> A good manager is best when people barely know that he exists. Not so good when people obey and acclaim him. Worse when they despise him.
> Tao Te Ching

Dictators never learn these lessons because they don't listen to people. You can end up very lonely if the only person you listen to is yourself. I am lucky in that I have no shortage of people prepared to tell me when I'm going off the track. My family and top management are great sounding boards, as are Mike and my board of directors. Everyone is likely to get off track and we need to know when it's happening, so welcome this advice when it's offered.

Personally, if somebody gives me a criticism, I like it. I find it a real positive, I really do. They have made me realise I can get too big for my boots. I think it is a very sad day in a person's life when they feel they're beyond criticism.

The delegator

Let's say you have a team of six to 12 and run a pretty tidy organisation. You work long hours and find the job pretty stressful, which is leading to health problems. The team works well if pushed, but you are not confident enough to let go the reins totally. You have tried to set up heads of department but find you step in and finish a lot of the jobs yourself. Your main concern is that if you don't keep on top of them and have your say and finish off many of the jobs for them, it won't be done as well and your job, or business, will be on the line.

The key is this: you have to empower your team and trust them. Make sure they are trained, know 100 per cent what is expected of them, and then let them go for it. Stepping in and finishing off for them undermines their position. They are no longer responsible for those actions because the buck now stops with you.

Until you stand back and observe your team in action, nothing will change. The secret is to observe and comment on a regular basis. At any sign of improvement, be lavish with your praise; if you are not satisfied, say so. Mistakes that are repeated require hard discipline or may even warrant a written warning. My rule of thumb is two-thirds praise, one-third correction and step heavily on repeated mistakes.

Running a successful business takes a strong discipline to stay focused on the long-term goals and objectives. If your team is fully behind that long-term vision, it will be much easier to maintain focus. Find a point of difference. What is it that makes you unique? Then share it with your people. Whether you employ two or 20,000, make sure they know without the slightest doubt where you are heading and what you expect from them. Once they have fully grasped that, empower them to take up their part of the challenge.

Now you watch, critique, praise, guide and listen to your people with little interference, keeping a steady eye on the target ahead. From this charged-up, passionate team will come innovative ideas, so listen.

I delegate. I always employ people that I know will be better than me and cover my weaknesses. They actually lift me up with them and make me stronger. Once you delegate and give people some responsibility, they strive to live up to it. They automatically think bigger.

Ironically, the bigger my company gets, the less I have to do. I can hand over all sorts of responsibilities to

> I always employ people that I know will be better than me and cover my weaknesses. **They actually lift me up with them.**

other people. Of course, I keep an eye on the big picture, but the real skill of delegation comes in choosing the right people.

Sometimes you choose the wrong person, and that person cannot grasp the art of delegating themselves. A telltale sign is the number of hours they work. I've never yet had anybody that works continuously more than 50 hours a week end up staying with us.

Never delegate to a dictator

Occasionally you're going to choose the wrong people, and I've had some disappointments. But I've chosen good people more often than bad ones.

People who are dishonest and not being true to themselves, or have an ulterior motive, can come unstuck. And that ulterior motive may be something as simple as worrying they will do themselves out of a job if they delegate to good people.

The Lazy Way to Success by Fred Gratzon

I can't claim to have achieved success by doing as little as successful businessman and transcendental meditation teacher Fred Gratzon advocates in his imaginative, counter-intuitive guide to success ... but I'm working on it.

Hard work, according to Gratzon, has nothing to do with success. In fact, it is counter-productive. Nature demonstrates this by always following the principle of least action — using the simplest action to achieve any result. People prove it in reverse because there are an awful lot of hard-working people in the world, but not that many successful ones.

'Success is inversely proportional to hard work,' says Gratzon.

The hardest work — any kind of physical labour — does not pay well. We need to use our brains to make money and find solutions that aren't exhausting. Most great advances — the wheel, fire, sails — were made by people looking for a way to do less, Gratzon notes.

Want to get something done? Do nothing. That's when the blinding flash of genius comes. If we let go consciously, the problem-solving process goes on under the surface.

He says the most effective way to motivate people is to get them to motivate themselves — for that, they need freedom, challenges, responsibility and a fun-filled environment. So don't treat work as work; treat it as play. If the leader is having a good time, everyone will want to get in on the act.

Too much, too soon

I know one person who treated his staff incredibly well. He gave them a trip, put them up in the best hotel, flew them around in a helicopter, had them playing golf at The Hills. It was a spectacular reward for the work they had done.

Within a year they had all gone, and it turned out they had been double-dealing behind his back, abusing their positions because he had so much money. So beware of giving out too much too soon, and test the waters thoroughly before jumping in.

When you delegate you have to factor that in. I usually go on my gut instinct to make the initial choice. After that, you can monitor people's performance one step at a time.

And I hope I give people inspiration so they want to prove they deserve the trust I put in them.

Be confident for them

The bigger the challenge you set a person, the more they are likely to rise to it. My head greenkeeper came from a neighbouring golf resort. He came by in the early days when I was forming the green in front of my new home. He couldn't help himself and started to lend a hand on his days off. We were doing the raking and shifting soil ourselves. We got on well and eventually he came to work for me.

I developed a goal for The Hills. I wanted to raise the bar. I wanted it to be not just a good course, but as good as it gets. It was pretty good, but I knew it could be better. I wasn't going to make this happen myself, so I delegated the job to my greenkeeper.

He was a little startled at first. But I sent him to look at a few courses overseas and now he knows just what we need to do to reach that first-class standard.

He also knows that once we have made The Hills the equal of any other course, we will be moving on to a new goal — making it better than any other course.

He had to work on his delegation because he had been used to doing a little bit of everybody's job, so now we have someone who's responsible for the greens, someone who's responsible for the fairway, someone who's responsible for the bunkers and someone who's responsible for the machinery.

All departments are covered and he is on top of his delegation, works fewer hours and achieves greater things. Since we made that adjustment the course has become even better, and the team are totally focused on and committed to the 30-year goal: making The Hills the best-presented course in the world — an audacious but achievable goal.

10. Think before you dig

Once, one of our senior people decided to dig his own swimming pool by hand. He didn't enjoy the digging. It wasn't some mad kind of exercise. And there was no way his time was worth less than it would have cost him to pay someone to dig his pool. But he went ahead and dug it anyway because he couldn't see that his time would have been used more productively and profitably — in every sense — on other things.

This story reminds me of a film I saw once, a black-and-white Japanese movie called *Woman in the Dunes*.

It was a film about the sort of traps people get themselves into. A woman lives at the bottom of a sandpit among some dunes. It can only be reached by a rope ladder but the others in the village have taken the ladder away. Her house keeps filling up with sand and she has to keep digging it out. She is joined by a man who gets trapped there and becomes her lover. He tries to get out at first but eventually gives up and becomes resigned to digging out the sand, day after day, just like her.

I think that film says it all.

We all have options.

Beware of doing repetitive jobs that lead you nowhere. I see it so often: people working on things that take them off the track to where they should be heading — their 30-year goal.

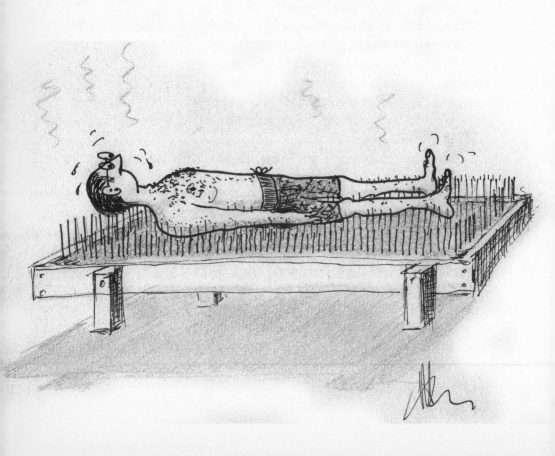

11. Change and chance, risks and mistakes

The most certain things in life are its uncertainties: change, chance, risks and mistakes. To think bigger successfully we have to learn not just to live with these but to harness them and use them to achieve great things.

I thrive on change, which is just as well because the world is changing much quicker than it used to. Some people think this is a purely modern phenomenon, but even back in the cave we would have to be prepared for rapid change. You never knew when that sabre-tooth tiger would put its head around the corner and bare its teeth.

People who fear change are really just afraid of the unknown

If they could see the future, and know what change was going to bring, they could prepare for it. Well, you can prepare for the future without knowing exactly what it will be.

I used to be terribly fearful of change because I couldn't see anything clearly. I had no goal and no vision. I genuinely could not see ahead because everything was in a permanent fog. I stayed in that fog in my uncle's shop for 23 years.

I tried to see through. I read all the books. I listened to the tapes. I went to seminars. The best I did was come up with a goal of doing a little property developing. I built some flats and started work on my own house. As you know, it was uncontrollable, unforeseeable change — that chance fire that burnt down my house — that cleared the fog away so I could see.

Until then I had almost certainly missed many chances that had come my way. I was oblivious to things. I didn't dare look at them, so I didn't know they were there. I had no more nor less talent and ability than anybody else. But if you can't see clearly, there is nothing to set your talents to work on.

Chances that are opportunities are like waves on the shore. They are constantly coming in and bombarding us. We can either run away so our feet don't get wet, or we can get out there with our surfboards and go for the most exhilarating ride. Clear the negative self-talk from the necktop computer and you are ready for anything.

It's not opportunism. It's not just taking the main chance or grabbing just anything that comes your way. It has to fit into a goal or a vision, which is why the goal or vision always comes before the opportunity.

America — land of opportunity

The decision to extend Michael Hill Jeweller to the USA was an extreme example of thinking bigger. No one from New Zealand had ever opened a chain of jewellery stores in Australia before we did. Yet we now have three times as many shops there as we do in New Zealand. And no Australasian jeweller had ever dared try to break into the US market before we did.

If you're going to THINK BIGGER you've got to push yourself, and that means you may have to accept some short-term discomfort. I want to take a chance, and make the most of it, so I'm setting up shop in the USA.

Have you ever swum competitively? Take the small-town high-school swimming champion who moves to the big city and trains harder and pretty soon is the best swimmer in that town. Finally he wins the nationals. Then he moves to Australia and his performance has to be good enough to compete internationally. He thought bigger and he got there.

When we opened in Canada, suddenly we were competing at a Commonwealth level. We trained harder and started to win races there. But by opening in Chicago we were sending a brand-new message: we want to win at the Olympics. We were pretty good swimmers by then, but I'm learning all sorts of new strokes and techniques now.

> # In the natural world some lose and in this way profit. Tao Te Ching

One of the best things about this has been that pushing ourselves this far has made a monumental difference to the core of the business, which would never have happened if we had not been thinking bigger.

It's made everyone in the company aware of a tougher world. We are determined. Many things have had to change. When it's so tough, you have to analyse your business from the core out. You have to work out what you stand for and redefine your point of difference.

As I write this, Canada is about to break even again after some ups and downs. That will give us energy to take south to Chicago where we are beefing up our training for the US pool.

We knew the look of our shops was not internationally competitive, so we have designed a new one. In the past, when we went for a new look, we just went ahead and built a store. That was a mistake. There would always be things wrong with the new design that you would only find out after all the work had been done. Then we would have to make big, expensive changes. This time we took a year to build the new store, starting with a prototype in our head office to experiment with and work out what was required.

We had to adapt for US conditions. The main issue was the lighting. Australasian lighting is quite bright and doesn't have much mood to it. In some clothing shops in North America and Europe, it's so dark that you feel the merchandise rather than look at it, but it creates a mood.

Not all the shops were in good locations. We have taken on a top leasing person and renegotiated the leases on all our shops. Some of them had to close because the landlords had us over a barrel with very high rentals they were not willing to budge on.

We have walked away from several locations, but the remainder, in excellent locations, will be getting the new look and we will be starting afresh. This will let us focus on stores that have the best chance of being turned around and making a profit. Then we will take these lessons and start applying them gradually across the USA — 1000 stores has never been more achievable than it is now.

As for our big point of difference, that is going to be our people in the long run. We have some wonderful talent who have given us insights into how Americans buy and think when they shop.

Many of the new lessons learnt in North America have given us insights into improvements and innovations in an Australasian setting, thereby giving us an edge over our competitors in this part of the world.

For example, in North America consumers like certificates and valuations on all their diamonds. They are more conscious of diamond grades.

We have adjusted the grade of diamonds we sell to be more internationally acceptable — cleaner white gems — and with our buying power increasing to purchases of more than $200 million per annum we are now in the league of the serious bidders.

So we started putting those diamond grades in our stores closer to home, and diamonds as a percentage of our total sales went way up. A survey was done recently that showed we were the most recognised jeweller now in Australasia.

I am feeling confident about entering a few more races in the swimming competition.

I have gone into so much detail about what we have done in America because I want to make clear that even with good goals, creative thinking and a readiness to embrace change, you still have to do the work.

It is easy, because it is solid, challenging fun.

Breaking into the North American market, we faced a whole range of problems and had to exert ourselves at every turn. We had to be realistic. We had to confront every aspect of the issue head on and find a solution. There always is a solution.

In our case, the result was a whole lot of solutions that are going to help us do even better in our older markets.

Plenty of people run very profitable businesses in the USA. The country is famous for it. We started on the back foot there because we didn't evolve in that culture. But, once again, the problem made things easier because it showed us where to focus our efforts.

In the move from New Zealand to Australia, we showed the Australians a thing or two — we were the first to have footpath blackboards outside the stores, and now everyone does; we were the first to discount as a matter of course, now numerous companies do.

In the move from Australia and New Zealand to North America, the Americans showed us an awful lot. I don't mind. I just want the best ideas — I don't care who had them first.

Toughened up

I spoke a lot in my last book about how an economic downturn provided a great opportunity for the tough to get going. It also demonstrated examples of the laws of unforeseen consequences, or serendipity, or it's an ill wind that blows no one any good. The phenomenon has many names, but despite all the difficulties we have stared down in the USA, we have had one great outcome.

Because of the downturn the US jewellery business almost completely collapsed, along with a lot of other retail businesses. As a consequence, we have been able to poach some of the very best jewellery retailers in the whole of the USA. We are overcapitalised with staff. We have all these great people waiting for their chance to show what they can do for us when things turn around. There's no end of people who want to make the business better.

If we had given up and packed up, we wouldn't have been able to use that opportunity. Instead, we saw a chance and we took it.

The biggest risk is doing nothing

There are risks with everything you do because events outside your control may be waiting to turn your world upside down. Thinking bigger means walking a tightrope, but the job of tightrope walker is nothing if not exciting.

So the worst risk is not to take any risks. You definitely won't fall off the tightrope, but you won't get to the other side either.

If you make a decision that doesn't work, you can try again. But if you make no decision then you'll never know. A lot of big organisations, particularly the sort that can get voted out or are vulnerable to industry politics, never take risks or make decisions. They are effectively — or rather, ineffectively — run by consultants, which is just an expensive way for some people to avoid responsibility. Nothing ever happens and the decision-making process goes around in big circles.

I will trust my intuition over a consultant any day. I believe consultants tell you what they think you want to hear.

When I take a risk it's an informed one. I've educated myself about the possible outcomes. And I take risks in areas I know about. I would never take what I call the retirement risk, like the farmer who decides he'll go and open a restaurant or plant a vineyard and then sit back to make some easy money. That 'retirement' is 20 times more difficult than the farming that they knew about.

All those principles about risk apply to other areas of life besides business.

If you were completely risk averse, you would never ask a girl out because you would be too worried she might say no. In that case, you would end up very lonely. Or you might not start a family because you thought it could go wrong. You have to have some faith in good outcomes even when you cannot control them 100 per cent.

If you've done your homework, practised and learnt some basic skills, at some stage you have to step out on the tightrope. Otherwise the person waiting behind you will push past and you'll be knocked to the ground.

12. Books that made a difference: 3

Out of Darkness by Zoltan Torey

This book is the autobiography of a man who was born in Hungary in 1929 but moved to Australia after World War II to escape Communism. While studying to be a dentist and working part time he was involved in a horrific accident where battery acid splashed in his face, blinding him. After recuperating he returned to university and graduated with honours in psychology and philosophy.

He has done major research on the brain, and his *The Crucible of Consciousness* was a breakthrough book about the problem of how consciousness works — how we are aware of our own thoughts. A few years later Torey published his autobiography, *Out of Darkness*, with a foreword by the great neurologist Oliver Sacks.

'From the moment his bandages come off he sets himself, with extraordinary tenacity, to taming his now heightened imagery, shaping it into a supple, reliable tool for living and thinking,' says Sacks. 'In doing so he not only compensates himself for the loss of his sight, but develops what is almost a new sense, a new faculty of mind.'

After the accident, Torey could not see anything — everything was totally black for the rest of his life. But in effect he taught himself to 'see without seeing'. It was as though he could see internally. He developed amazing powers of visualisation, so strong that he was asked to help find faults in cars. It was as though he could send his mind into engines and have a good look around. He travelled and watched television and even mended his rooftop guttering.

From a chance event, a major life change, Torey developed strengths that have bypassed the negatives and, if anything, probably made him more determined to succeed.

Life

Those who are firm and inflexible are in harmony with dying. Those who are yielding and receptive are in harmony with living. The position of the highly inflexible will descend; the position of the yielding and receptive will ascend.

Tao Te Ching

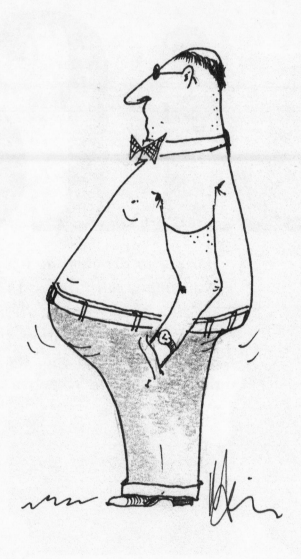

1. Prognosis: Good

A healthier life

It would be disappointing to not take up this opportunity life has given you to achieve everything and anything — including wealth, happiness and health.

If we work on your characteristics holistically, we can develop you into a complete package, so you can stop having to push and struggle to get ahead and be effortlessly magnetised to a higher level of awareness and achievement.

Health is such an important part of thinking bigger that I am going to give you a lot to think about. So please stick with me and read all this section. I have once again applied the 80/20 rule and concentrated on the 20 per cent of the major issues that I see need addressing.

You only get one shot at life so make the most of it by staying fit, trim and being aware of the foods, vitamins and hormones that can keep us in peak performance.

My advice might seem too hard or fanatical. I'm sure you can think of many reasons to shirk this section, but once you get into the swing of this approach to health, you will feel a hell of a lot better and much more able to think bigger.

Water you waiting for?

The first step to keeping a healthy body is to drink plenty of pure water. Three-quarters of your brain is water, 70 per cent of your muscle, 82 per cent of your blood — so nourish those vital components by drinking eight glasses a day.

It is important to know what sort of water to drink as most of it is polluted. Most drinking water from bores, wells or springs is derived from surface or ground water. This run-off water is rarely pure as it is contaminated by agriculture: pesticides and fertilisers. Town-supply water is no better as it usually contains chlorine and sometimes fluoride.

The only reliable way to be sure what you're drinking is pure water is to drink distilled bottled water or, better still, install your own home water distiller. There are plenty available on the internet that will provide you with clean, pure water. Carbon and other water filters are not effective.

Some critics argue that drinking pure water will deprive you of important minerals. But the good news is that all the minerals and vitamins we need come from the fruit, vegetables and grains we consume. If we had to rely on minerals from water, the minuscule amount we would receive would leave us in bad shape.

Going up in smoke?

If we wish to become very serious about achieving our 30-year goal, there is one habit that needs to be kicked — smoking. It accounts for about a third of all cancer deaths. Lung cancer is fatal in more than 80 per cent of cases, and the news for those exposed to second-hand smoke is nearly as bad.

According to Dr Michael Colgan, a best-selling author and nutritionist who has given me excellent health advice over the years, non-smoking women have a 24 per cent increased risk of lung cancer over their lifetime if their partner is a smoker. This risk increases with the number of cigarettes smoked and the duration of the relationship.

Fortunately, the habit never worked for me. I tried and bought a pipe and loose tobacco, but I could never keep it alight. The packing of tobacco was a skill I never mastered. Christine smoked when I met her — around three or four a day — but gave up when the children were on the way. Her father smoked a pipe and one night in front of the fire, he said aloud, 'This is bloody ridiculous', and threw into the flames all his pipes, cleaners, pouches and tobacco. He never smoked again!

Smoking is linked with some 40 diseases — so give it up. Dr Colgan has heard it from hundreds of patients: 'I'm in great shape, Doc. A few ciggies won't hurt.' Don't you believe it. Good nutrition, regular exercise and fitness cannot protect you if you continue to smoke. You cannot get away with it. Please set your goals and then take immediate steps to quit.

As a last resort, check into a substance abuse clinic to help you stop. If you don't heed this advice to protect your health, everything else you read from here on is a waste of time.

Please do it.

To sleep, perchance to achieve a 30-year goal

To think bigger we need to get our sleep. The body needs a minimum of eight or nine hours' rest a night to recuperate from its day's activities. Your body is intricate and complex, like a helicopter or any complicated flying machine. You can run it for days, but when it's in the workshop for maintenance, a team of mechanics and technicians painstakingly check each piece of equipment and replace worn parts. Your body is no different.

To do a warrant of fitness, the team come in at night and replace parts, clean out unwanted bits, check the wiring and plumbing, and remove any unwanted viruses or potentially damaging diseases. You can run on less sleep, sure. I have friends who thrive on five or six hours and seem as bright as a kitten — off to bed after partying until midnight and up again for a six o'clock start. It seems to work for them year after year.

But it's like an unserviced helicopter or other aircraft. Some seem to keep going regardless, but there will always come a time when things go wrong. The unserviced aircraft eventually malfunctions, with serious consequences.

Without its eight hours' daily self-maintenance, the body leaves some jobs uncompleted, and over time these small faults develop into a major disease, stroke or heart attack.

So the golden rule is: early to bed, early to rise, keeps you happy, healthy and wise.

Melatonin, a natural hormonal cascade produced in the pineal gland and other organs, replenishes our bodies at night while our eyes are closed, but as we age past 40, our levels decline. That is why older people have difficulty sleeping. To aid sleep and replenish my body with antioxidants, I take three milligrams of natural slow-release melatonin in tablet form at bedtime. I recommend getting your doctor to check out your hormone levels and keeping your melatonin levels up where they should be, so you get your eight hours of sound sleep.

2. Young for life

It's never too late

Rose Blumkin was born in Russia and migrated to the United States of America during World War II. She settled in Nebraska and had difficulty getting work because of her broken English. Eventually she got a job in retail and before long wanted to set up her own furniture store. However, it was difficult as no one would give her credit and no one wanted to supply her wholesale. Undeterred, she set off for New York and acquired furniture, at retail price less a discount. This was the start of the Nebraska Furniture Mart, in a small insignificant building.

It was an instant success. She acquired credit and started to buy at wholesale prices. Over her lifetime, she grew this tiny store into a gigantic organisation that covered 72 acres — the longest furniture mart in all of the United States. One day, the famous American investor Warren Buffett, who lived in the area, walked into the store and asked Mrs B, as he called her, how much she would sell for. She said $60 million and he accepted on the spot, provided she and her family stayed to run the business, which they agreed to do.

At the age of 94 her nephews, whom she had groomed into the business, in their wisdom decided it was time for Mrs B to retire. They gave her a great send-off, with flowers, cakes and a large celebration. However, Mrs B was not that comfortable with the thought of retirement so she decided to set up business across the road in opposition. Over the next few years she grew her carpet mart to be the third-biggest in the United States. She was starting to hurt business across the road.

Warren Buffet, who had bought the business before her retirement, was shocked when she opened up in opposition to him across the road. He had made one of the few mistakes in his lifetime — he didn't think he needed to get Mrs B to sign a restraint of trade because she was so old. Eventually Warren Buffet went cap in hand to Mrs B and arranged to buy out her carpet mart as well. Mrs B once again went back and ran the original Nebraska Furniture Mart until she died at the age of 104.

I started Michael Hill Jeweller when I was 40. Georgio Armani started his business at 41. Ray Kroc started McDonald's at 52. But Mrs B started hers at 94. So remember . . . it's never too late to set goals and start a business.

Age is largely in the mind. We tell ourselves that we cannot do certain things at certain times because of a number on a calendar. There's no reason why we can't keep performing to a high standard, working towards goals at any age, if we have the desire and the health. Having a goal in itself helps to keep us young.

How we have programmed the necktop computer has a huge impact on how we age. We might have let it completely seize up by late middle age. But we now know that we can keep our minds and our bodies in good shape. We don't have to suffer the negative effects of ageing that were unavoidable in the past.

It's never too late to set goals and start a business – Mrs B started hers at 94.

There's proof of the benefits of a good old age in the large number of people who came into their own later in life. Architect Frank Lloyd Wright was doing some of his best work in his 80s. So was the sculptor Auguste Rodin. The painter Michelangelo died in his 90s when most people of his era didn't make it to their mid-30s. And I wrote earlier about how Stradivari's violin-making skills kept developing so extraordinarily until he was over 90.

Those are a few examples of people who managed to resist being brainwashed into acting old in days gone by. They were exceptions in their time. But today we have a big advantage over them. We have the benefit of bio-identical hormone therapy, of which I have become a firm adherent. It keeps you younger and it keeps everything working.

We have a very real choice now: we can either live in the dark and not try these things, or we can take advantage of these wonderful breakthroughs in longevity medicine.

70 60 50 40 30

3. Books that made a difference: 4

Ageless by Suzanne Somers

Our internal organs and hormones don't have to be as old as the date on our birth certificates. *Ageless* discusses bio-identical hormones — natural hormones made from soy and yams — taken as supplements when our own hormone levels start to decline, which the author believes can turn back the years. Traditional hormone replacement therapy, once popular as a treatment for women in menopause, fell out of favour when research showed the synthetic hormones being used had serious negative side effects.

It seems that the pharmaceutical industry doesn't want you to know about bio-identical hormones because they are natural substances and therefore can't be patented — and therefore can't make money for the drug companies.

We are being artificially aged by the number of chemicals and toxins in our environment. So it makes sense to do what we can to counter these effects.

Previously, people died before their hormones started to run down. Thanks to technology, we are now living past that age. Once hormone levels go down, the brain regards the body as unproductive and lets it run down. Bio-identical hormone replacement therapy (BHRT) restores hormones to their optimal levels and tricks the brain into thinking the body is still reproductive.

In this way we can say goodbye to what Somers calls the seven dwarfs of menopause: Itchy, Bitchy, Sweaty, Sleepy, Bloated, Forgetful and All-Dried-Up.

To those who criticise this practice as 'not natural', I say (with Somers) it's not natural to have an artificial hip, contact lenses or heart bypass surgery — but no one would turn down those life-saving or life-enhancing options.

While women have long had to learn to deal with menopause, we are only just beginning to understand that there is a male equivalent — andropause — in which men's levels of testosterone, the steroid DHEA and growth hormone steadily decline. It takes longer than menopause and is therefore not as noticeable, but it is real and effects include low energy, fatigue, osteoporosis, enlarged prostate, depression, anxiety, less strong or infrequent erections and even impotence. The correct bio-identical hormones can reduce or reverse these effects. Men need testosterone, oestrogen, progesterone and thyroid in the correct balance for optimal hormone health.

Another important anti-ageing strategy with a hormone connection is getting enough sleep. People do best if they go to bed between 9 pm and 10 pm, giving your hormones time to 'catch up'. Our sleep patterns were established before there were artificial lights, so we really are designed to sleep when it's dark — cortisol levels drop during the day, leading to lowered insulin levels. These go up again when the sun comes up, giving us alertness and energy.

Stress also prematurely ages us. Calmness keeps you young; hence the importance of meditation, which is discussed in another part of this book, to keep down our levels of cortisol, the stress hormone. Regular exercise also helps lower stress. (If you don't have time to exercise, think again as the alternatives are not good.) Even keeping a journal — writing out our worries — helps lower cortisol.

People do best if they go to bed between 9 pm and 10 pm.

Diet is also essential for hormone health. We need to eat real food, not food that's artificially flavoured and full of pesticides, salt and sugar. 'Sugary foods and trans fats disrupt your hormones,' says Somers, 'so they can no longer keep your body on an even keel to give you the youthful energy and health that you want.'

However, it's unlikely you will be able to get all the vitamins and minerals you need from the food you eat so it's also important to take supplements for optimal health. I particularly like the attitude to nature expressed by Dr Paul Schulick, quoted in *Ageless*:

> We lack a sense of deep connectiveness with the earth. When I'm in Costa Rica or when I'm taking a walk in the woods, there are literally thousands of life forms all around me, chirping and singing. You feel such a oneness with the force of creation that it's almost impossible to be depressed or feel a lack of energy. But in today's world, we live in self-imposed cages. We don't get out enough. We don't experience the force of nature. As a result, I think we are like animals in a zoo ... Why does everybody go to the beach? What is it about the beach that attracts people? It's the primal force of creation. We just need more of that. It is in our natures.

Bio-identical hormone replacement therapy is a huge anti-ageing opportunity — the free fountain of youth that can keep your insides going. What an opportunity we have here.

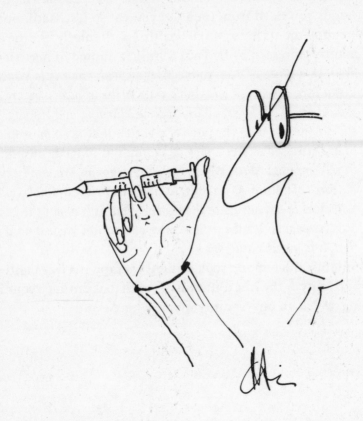

4. On not ageing

My advice is to arrange to have annual blood tests from your GP.

I'd do anything to not have to have blood taken. What's wrong with my self-programming? I sweat when the nurse puts the needle in. I go hot and cold and usually afterwards the nurse has to ask if I am OK. I may have to lie down. Rather pathetic, I grant you, but regardless I still get them done. I see them as like a chart of where my health is heading, and to achieve our long-term goal we need to be sure we're heading down the right path for optimum health. So have a complete blood test done once a year. You will need a blood test form from your doctor indicating the test required. Do not eat from 10 pm the night before until after you have had the test the next morning, but drink plenty of water.

The tests will be analysed and the appropriate vitamins and minerals prescribed for any deficiencies. Would you drive your car for years without having it checked?

> We run out of hormones as an accident of our living longer.

A lot of New Zealanders are deficient in vitamin D, zinc, magnesium and iodine. If you're mineral deficient, your body will be out of sync.

So don't wait until your minerals or natural hormone levels start to run down if you want to stay in optimum health.

For more information, email rosi@drrosi.com or check out www.colganinstitute.com and also www.A4m.org

5. Think smaller — food that makes a champion

A healthy diet is an essential part of work-life balance. Food is the fuel for the good health without which we cannot achieve anything. We need nutritious food to let us think bigger.

At the same time, of course, food is also one area where we want to think *smaller*. The obesity epidemic in the Western world is startling to behold. It's hard to see how anyone can pursue a goal with any energy or hope of success when they are carting around excess weight equal to that of a small pony. Their mass slows them down and decreases their life expectancy — so much for 30-year goals.

Many people might regard my own eating as 'austere' and 'no fun'. I believe this is a misconception based on outdated ways of thinking about food. Our palates have been severely abused by sugars and salts and trans fats, not just in fast food and snacks but in calorie-laden 'gourmet' food as well. We need to be re-educated to appreciate food that is prepared in a healthy manner.

'I don't like that salady stuff. I can't eat this green shit — I just don't like the taste of it. It's not for me. I like a big steak,' was one reaction from someone who once came on our boat with us.

But you're the one who decides whether or not you like certain foods. I find it no trouble to adjust to any taste of food, really; it's a mindset. You can tell yourself that you like it. There are very few foods I couldn't train myself to like. So I must admit to being unable to understand people who turn up their noses and say, 'Eww, that healthy food, can't stand it. Tastes like nothing.'

Is it because their taste buds have been so abused, they cannot actually tell what something tastes like? When you think about it, we must have evolved to like the taste of healthy food as that gave us a chance of survival. I find it fun to try a different food, knowing it's going to be good for me. Food is an aesthetic experience as well. Food is for the senses what music is for the ear. You have to think bigger than merely saying 'This tastes terrible' when the consequences of an unhealthy diet are even more terrible.

Food is an aesthetic experience as well. **Food is for the senses what music is for the ear.**

This is an area where I can speak from a lot of experience: I have tried so many diets. There was the Ross Horne diet. He was a fruitarian and on his diet you eat only fruit, vegetables, nuts and seeds. There was the Pritikin Diet, which focused on natural whole foods, and the Russian Diet, a low-calorie, low-carb regime — millet, green shakes.

It has all been part of trying to find the healthiest nutrition possible. If you don't experiment you'll never make any progress. Based on my experiences with food, I've come up with a basic meal plan that I follow. On top of this there are Christine's wonderful recipes. When you eat out, if you know a little bit about food, you can usually find a reasonably healthy option on a menu.

Breakfast

I won't eat any of the mass-produced cereals because they're absolutely full of everything that's wrong. They will dose you with massive amounts of sugar and salt, which is going to be terrible for you and put on excess, unwanted weight.

The best thing I've discovered to start the day is fruit. Whole fruit is best — not those pre-cut pieces of fruit you find in the supermarket. Once food is cut it starts to lose nutrients straight away. And not stewed fruit, as it is usually full of sugar. Even in a hotel anywhere around the world, there will usually be whole fruit available for breakfast. Whether it's whole, pesticide-free, organic fruit is another matter, but it's better than a chocolate cereal or sausages and bacon.

The other acceptable choice for breakfast is porridge (organic rolled oats). That is also usually available in hotels if you're travelling. I soak my oatmeal overnight in water. (I use distilled water because the water quality is so variable wherever you go. All the fertiliser that goes on the land doesn't get filtered out and some of it ends up in the water, so you have to distil.) I add some raisins and flaxseed oil.

Lunch on the road

I used to love canned baked beans. They're often touted as health food: vegetarian and high in protein and fibre. But if you look at the ingredients list on the tin, you will find you're also eating a huge amount of sugar and salt. People think they're having a healthy lunch but it's quite the opposite. Tragically, canned baked beans are out.

I've never been one for lunching in a restaurant if I can avoid it. For lunch if we are away, Christine and I usually go to a supermarket and buy tomatoes, avocados, sprouts, a lettuce and smoked salmon. Sardines in spring water are also good. I'll put it in a thin wrap. And then you can go out with your little pocket knife in your bag, find somewhere pleasant and sit there enjoying the food and each other's company, knowing you're eating well.

We've always done that. A lot of people are surprised that we actually make our own lunch. I think they expect us to have a chef on hand to prepare meals according to our latest whim. But preparing your own food is good for your head. It keeps you a little bit in touch with nature wherever you are. It's the life part of the work-life balance.

That also raises the point that if you can buy your food close to the time you eat it, then it won't have lost

> **If you can buy your food close to the time you eat it, then it won't have lost so many nutrients.**

so many nutrients from having been stored. Also, the closer you buy it to the place where it was grown, the better it will be for you because it won't have come as far to reach your plate.

That said, frozen vegetables are a good alternative if you can't get fresh. They are often 'fresher' when you eat them than something you buy that has been sitting in a shop for several days.

Dinner

Steam everything — it will surprise you. One of the simplest and healthiest methods of food preparation is steaming using an old-fashioned Chinese bamboo steamer. These simple cooking tools cost only a few dollars but their health benefits are priceless.

Steaming retains the food's nutrients. There's no need for any fat and you can flavour anything simply with garlic, ginger, chilli or herbs. If you're worried about the amount of salt you consume (you should be), you can start gradually reducing the amount you include in your cooking. After a few weeks, the salt will be almost eliminated from your diet and you won't even notice the difference.

Steaming is a fabulous way to cook fish or a whole chicken.

Steaming is a fabulous way to cook fish or a whole chicken. I love chicken, but once again, there's good chicken and bad chicken. Buy hormone-free. Similar precautions are necessary with fish. Swordfish or other very large fish, unfortunately, will be likely to contain mercury, so we probably need to leave those alone as well.

What not to eat

Say no to the dessert trolley, as it's a sure-fire way to add inches to the waistline and cause serious health problems. Be strong. If you must, it's best to go for a fruit platter or finish with dark chocolate. Buy chocolate containing 80-85 per cent pure chocolate cocoa.

Cocoa is full of polyphenol, a powerful antioxidant that protects your arteries. The best way to eat it is to place a piece under the tongue and suck it slowly to absorb it. We want no clogged-up, plaque-filled veins here, so lay off the creams and finish with quality chocolate instead.

But, if you absolutely have to have a dessert:

Lesley Colgan's Raspberry Cream Delight
Serves 4 to 6
Ingredients
  3 cups fresh organic raspberries
  2 cups low-fat vanilla quark or sugar-free yoghurt
  ½ cup ion exchange whey protein concentrate
  1 tbsp freshly squeezed lemon juice
  1 tbsp Barlean's flax oil

Purée raspberries in a blender, then sieve to remove seeds. Blend quark, protein concentrate, lemon juice and flax oil until smooth. Add raspberry purée.
Put in an ice-cream maker and freeze.

What not to drink

One of the biggest problems we face is obesity, even in young children. One of the key contributors can be regularly drinking soft drinks and sodas. That supersize cola or lemonade is giving you a mountain of refined white sugar that will have an immediate effect on your waistline and your chances of becoming a diabetic, or getting cancer or coronary disease. And forget the diet soft drinks as these contain artificial chemicals that have other long-term side effects.

Don'ts

We don't eat any fried food. We don't eat any battered food. As for fish and chips — I wouldn't let them put in a deep fryer at The Hills clubhouse because the oil is treated to keep it from going rancid and it's full of trans fats, so will clog your arteries big time. The body doesn't know how to handle trans fats so they go straight into your pipes.

Any soft drinks are totally no-nos. There's not one soft drink out there that's worth drinking, and don't bother with packaged fruit juices either. Many aren't even 100 per cent juice and most have added sugar. Forget about your orange juice in the morning unless it's squeezed naturally. You're better to drink water.

A voice of reason

I have recently been introduced to the writing of American food authority Michael Pollan. His simple little book *Food Rules* contains 64 guidelines for good eating. It uses very few words to convey some age-old wisdom about food. Some of his witty and common-sense rules include:

Don't eat anything your great-grandmother wouldn't recognise as food.

Avoid foods that have some form of sugar or sweetener listed among the top three ingredients.

Stop eating before you're full and try to eat only up to 80 per cent capacity.

Don't get your 'fuel' from the same place your car does.

Do all your eating at a table, not at a desk, while working, watching television or driving.

Eat food cooked by humans, not corporations.

Don't eat anything with more than five ingredients. (That one really struck a chord with me — so many so-called health foods actually have all sorts of extra additives that are no good for you.)

You could usefully contemplate those simple techniques and know pretty much all you need to know about how to eat well and healthily.

In the spirit of the advice outlined above, and in order to supplement my basic suggestions for breakfast, lunch and dinner, on the following pages you will find The Christine Hill (Miniature) Recipe Book — some of our favourite, healthy dishes, none of which break any of Pollan's rules and all of which are guaranteed delicious.

To whet your appetite, and get the day off to a good start, here is Dr Michael Colgan's Essential Muesli — it's got essential fats, whole grains and nutrients that increase their absorption.

Dr Michael Colgan's Essential Muesli
Serves 4
Ingredients
   4 tbsp pumpkin seeds
   4 tbsp sesame seeds
   4 tbsp sunflower seeds
   4 tbsp flaxseeds
   2 tbsp almonds with skins
   4 cups rolled oats
   ½ cup fresh non-sweetened apple juice
   cinnamon to taste
   1 cup fresh fruit
   1 cup plain low-fat unsweetened yoghurt

Grind seeds lightly in a coffee grinder. Chop almonds.
Combine nuts and seeds with oats.
Stir in apple juice. Add cinnamon and fresh fruit.
Let stand five minutes, then top with yoghurt and serve.

6. The Christine Hill
(Miniature) Recipe Book

My wife Christine has agreed to write out some of our favourite healthy recipes, so that you can put into practice the dietary and nutritional advice in this book. Some of these are ethnic dishes from around the world. Others have been refined by her over the years to suit our taste and lifestyle. But all are health-giving and prove that food that is good for you is anything but boring.

Christine's Amazing Wild Stinging Nettle Soup

This soup is very delicious and unusual — and a marvellous green colour. Pick large bunches of the soft leaves of spring stinging nettles. You will need to wear rubber gloves.

Ingredients

nettles

onion and garlic

olive oil

2 large potatoes

boiling water

homemade chicken stock (optional), fat removed

ground black pepper

nutmeg

1 poached egg to float in each bowl — you only need to do this if serving a special dinner.

Wash nettles well and discard thick stalks (use your gloves). Fry chopped onion and garlic in a large pan in a small amount of olive oil.

Add nettle leaves and peeled and diced potatoes. Add water and chicken stock to almost cover.

Add pepper and nutmeg.

Simmer 20-30 minutes.

Blend using a hand-held blender.

The soft poached egg floated on top of each bowl looks amazing.

Mediterranean Bean Soup

Ingredients

1 onion and 3 cloves of garlic, chopped

2 tablespoons olive oil

4 peeled tomatoes (or 1 can tomatoes)

3–4 sticks chopped celery plus leaves

1 large chopped carrot

1 cup black-eyed beans (they don't need soaking) or can of butter or cannellini beans

6 whole allspice, ground

1 fresh chopped chilli

ground black pepper

boiling water

1 tsp brown sugar

Parmesan and paprika to serve

Lightly fry onion and garlic in a small amount of oil. Add remaining vegetables, beans and spices, plus another 2 tbsp oil. Add boiling water to cover and brown sugar. Stir, then simmer until vegetables are cooked. Serve in wide bowls with a sprinkling of Parmesan and paprika.

Fresh Organic Silverbeet and Lentil Soup

Ingredients

1 onion, chopped

2 cloves garlic, chopped

olive oil

1 bunch organic silverbeet, roughly chopped

1 large cup red lentils

boiling water

ground black pepper

grated nutmeg

non-fat unsweetened yoghurt

chopped parsley to garnish

Fry onion and garlic in a large pan using a small amount of olive oil.
Add chopped silverbeet and stir-fry for a few minutes.
Add lentils and water to almost cover.
Add black pepper and nutmeg.
Simmer 20–30 minutes.
Blend with a hand-held blender.
Serve in wide bowls with spoonful of yoghurt on top and parsley for garnish.

Moroccan Carrot and Harissa

Ingredients

4 large carrots, peeled and roughly chopped

1 tsp harissa (chilli paste available at delicatessens)

⅓ cup virgin olive oil

ground black pepper

2 cloves garlic, chopped

Cook carrots until tender. Drain well and while still warm put into a food processor and process until smooth. Add harissa and re-blend with olive oil, pepper and garlic.

Middle Eastern Hummus (a variation)

Ingredients

1 can organic garbanzo beans (chick peas) (or ½ cup of dry garbanzo beans, soaked overnight in water, then boiled for 30–45 minutes until soft)

1 crushed garlic clove

¼ cup organic tahina paste (sesame seed paste)

organic olive oil

organic pumpkin seed oil

juice of ½ lemon

¼ tsp each ground coriander, cumin, paprika

pinch cayenne pepper

chopped spring onions

chopped parsley to garnish

Using a blender or food processor, blend beans, garlic, then add tahina, oils and lemon juice until it is a coarse paste. Add some water if mixture is too thick. Add spices and blend in a food processor. Transfer to a bowl and stir in chopped spring onions. Garnish with parsley to serve as a dip or for use in wraps.

Yummy Steamed Broccoli Salad

Ingredients
broccoli
red onion

Dressing
2 tbsp virgin olive oil
2 tbsp lemon juice
1 tsp ground cumin
¼ cup flat leaf parsley chopped
1 clove garlic chopped
ground black pepper

Lightly steam broccoli and roughly chop.
Dice red onion.
Toss broccoli and onion together. Combine all dressing ingredients and add to salad.

Christine's Cabbage Salad

Ingredients
½ cabbage, finely shredded
1 red onion, cut into fine circles
pinch Himalayan mineral salt
1 heaped tsp caraway seeds

Dressing
virgin olive or flaxseed oil
malt vinegar
½ tsp Dijon mustard

Combine salad ingredients and toss with combined dressing ingredients.
You can add other vegetables to liven up the cabbage — watercress leaves, chopped celery or walnuts are good.

Raw Beetroot and Carrot Salad
Serves 2

Ingredients
1 fresh raw beetroot
1 large carrot
chopped spring onion
chopped parsley or coriander
dry-roasted pine nuts and/or
sunflower, sesame or pumpkin seeds

Dressing
1 tbsp virgin olive oil
½ tbsp concentrated apple juice
½ tbsp pomegranate molasses
½ tbsp malt vinegar

Grate beetroot and carrot. Roughly mix in a salad bowl, then add remaining vegetables. Combine dressing ingredients and pour over salad. Sprinkle with the nuts.

Middle Eastern Spinach in Filo Pastry

Ingredients
1 onion
1 bunch fresh spinach
1 egg
Parmesan
feta or goat's cheese
filo pastry

Preheat oven to 170°C.
Chop onion to fine dice in food processor. Remove to a bowl. Chop spinach in food processor, small amounts at a time. Mix with onion. Add beaten egg, then a small quantity of cheese. Fold a strip of filo lengthwise. Place a large spoonful of spinach mixture in one corner and fold on the diagonal to make triangular parcels. Alternatively, make into one large pie using two sheets of filo for the base and two for the top, folded into a large parcel. Bake for 30-45 minutes.

Courgette Omelette Cake
(Christine made this for me when we first met.)

Ingredients

3-4 courgettes, grated

2 beaten eggs

bunch chopped dill (or dill seed if fresh unavailable)

½ cup currants

ground pepper

Put grated courgettes in a bowl and mix in other ingredients. Lightly grease a fry pan with a smear of olive oil and heat. Pour in mixture and cook on gentle heat for 10 minutes when it will be easy to turn over. Cook for a few minutes on the other side. Turn out onto a serving plate. Great for lunch with a salad.

Lebanese Eggplant and Yoghurt

Ingredients

1 large eggplant

virgin olive oil

pine nuts

½ clove crushed garlic

½ cup plain unsweetened yoghurt

Halve and slice eggplant and lightly fry in a little olive oil. Place on a serving platter. Roast pine nuts in a hot fry pan. Mix crushed garlic into yoghurt and pour over eggplant while it is still warm. Sprinkle pine nuts over.

Fennel, Feta and Pomegranate Salad
Serves 8 as a side dish

Ingredients

3 fennel bulbs

1 bunch of asparagus

2 tbsp olive oil

3 tbsp rapeseed oil

juice of 2 lemons

5 tsp sumac

black pepper and salt if desired

200g feta cheese

4 tbsp chervil leaves

3 tbsp parsley leaves

4 tbsp tarragon leaves

4 tbsp chives, cut into 3cm sticks

1 pomegranate, seeds removed

Cut the fennel bulbs into 3mm slices. Thinly slice the asparagus on an angle.
In a bowl, mix the oils, lemon juice, sumac and seasoning. Add the fennel and mix well. Layer the fennel, asparagus and crumbled feta on a serving platter. Sprinkle over the herbs, pomegranate seeds and the rest of the dressing.

Mark Hill's Rabbit in Red Wine

Ingredients

1 rabbit, wild caught if possible
rice flour
dry mustard
dry or fresh tarragon
virgin olive oil
2 large onions, chopped
red wine
1 bunch parsley

Preheat oven to 160°C.
Joint the rabbit and dust pieces in flour mixed with dry mustard and tarragon.
Sear in a hot pan using a small amount of olive oil. Remove to a casserole dish.
Fry onion in pan. Remove and place in casserole with rabbit joints.
Sprinkle small amount of flour into pan juices and stir for a few minutes. Add red wine, stir into flour mixture and cook together to make a sauce.
Add sauce to rabbit and throw in chopped parsley.
Cover and put in slow oven (160°C) for 2 hours or until rabbit is tender. Check occasionally to make sure it has not dried out — if it has, add a little more wine.

Greek Prawns and Feta Cheese à la Christine

Ingredients

10 prawns, preferably wild caught but frozen is OK if Australian

8 chopped spring onions

virgin olive oil

4 peeled and chopped tomatoes

large bunch parsley, chopped

½ cup white wine

feta or goat's cheese

ground black pepper

Preheat oven to 200°C.
Peel and de-vein prawns.
Fry spring onions in a little oil.
Add tomatoes and parsley and cook for 5 minutes.
Add white wine and simmer for 10 minutes. Season with pepper.
Pour a layer of tomato mix into an ovenproof dish. Add prawns, then remaining tomato mix.
Crumble feta on top.
Bake for 10 minutes or until prawns are pink.
Serve with rice, couscous or quinoa.

My Favourite Fish Fillets in Filo Pastry

Ingredients

bunch of spinach

1 small cup non-fat cottage cheese

squeeze of lemon juice

filo pastry (can be used straight from the packet and doesn't need to be brushed with oil or butter)

fish fillets (blue cod is good)

ground black pepper

1 egg, beaten (optional)

Preheat oven and oven tray to 170°C.
Put spinach in a food processor and chop finely. Mix in cottage cheese and lemon juice.
Use 2 sheets of filo per fillet.
Lay fish on pastry and top with spinach mixture and pepper.
Fold into individual fish parcels.
Place parcels on hot tray. Brush with beaten egg if desired.
Bake 20-30 minutes.

Christine's Organic Whole Chicken Cooked in Bamboo Steamer

Ingredients
1 whole organic chicken

bay leaves

favourite stuffing

3 Stuffings
Chopped onion, thyme and parsley, chopped garlic, chopped prunes and black pepper.

Half an onion (chopped), half a lemon or preserved lemon (chopped), bay leaf and garlic.

Chopped onion, celery, dried apricots, garlic and fresh herbs.

Lightly fry choice of ingredients in virgin olive oil.

Dry and stuff the chicken with one of these stuffings. Tie up legs, wings and cavity.

Put whole chicken on back in bamboo steamer. Layer a few bay leaves on the breast.

Place steamer on wok or large pan filled with water. Steam chicken for 1½-2 hours.

Juices will fall into the water. Cool, remove fat and use as chicken stock.

Dr Colgan's Lip-Smacking Lemon Chicken

Ingredients

½ cup freshly squeezed lemon juice

1 clove garlic, chopped

pinch pepper

4 fresh boneless organic chicken breasts, hormone-free

3 sprigs fresh rosemary

1 lemon, thinly sliced

Combine lemon juice, garlic and pepper.

Place chicken in one layer on bottom of shallow dish.

Pour juice mixture over chicken and turn to thoroughly coat both sides.

Pull rosemary needles off sprigs and sprinkle over chicken.

Let stand for 15 minutes.

Grill chicken under high heat for about 5 minutes per side, until meat at centre is no longer pink.

Garnish with lemon slices and serve.

Christine's Favourite Fish, Garlic and Rosemary

Ingredients

fillets of any firm white fish (blue cod, grouper, snapper, etc.)

1 tbsp rice flour mixed with 1 tsp paprika

virgin olive oil

4 cloves garlic, finely sliced

fresh rosemary

½ cup red wine vinegar

parsley to garnish

Dust fish fillets in flour/paprika mixture. Lightly fry in small amount of olive oil and set aside. Fry garlic slices and rosemary in remaining oil in skillet until golden. Add red wine vinegar. Stir until well mixed and pour over fish fillets. Garnish with chopped parsley.

VvS1 Salmon with Mushroom Dressing

VvS1 is a diamond term meaning clarity is nearly but not quite perfect.

Ingredients

1 cup chopped spring onions

2 cups thinly sliced field mushrooms

2 tbsp virgin olive oil

2 cloves garlic

¼ cup chopped fresh dill or fennel

juice of ½ lemon

salt (Himalayan mineral salt)

freshly ground black pepper

1 large papaya, sliced (or apricots or nectarines if papaya unavailable)

1 tbsp white wine vinegar

fillet of fresh salmon

1 lemon, finely sliced

Preheat oven to 180-200°C. Combine spring onions, mushrooms, oil, garlic, dill, lemon juice, and salt and pepper. Let stand at least 5 minutes. Combine fruit with vinegar and more salt and pepper. Let stand at least 5 minutes. Place salmon fillet in a shallow ovenproof dish, skin down. Pour over mushroom mixture and arrange lemon slices on top. Bake 20 mins. Transfer to a serving dish and garnish with papaya mixture.

VvS1 Fish with Tomato Dressing

Ingredients

3 tomatoes, finely diced

½ cucumber, peeled and diced

1 red onion, peeled and diced

few sprigs of dill or fennel, chopped

1 tbsp flax oil or virgin olive oil

1 tbsp organic pumpkin seeds

½ cup rice vinegar or white wine vinegar

½ cup fresh lemon juice

any type of firm-fleshed white fish (blue cod, mahi mahi, snapper, grouper)

Combine sauce ingredients and let stand 30–60 minutes in refrigerator.

Dry-grill or steam fish. Cooking time depends on fish type and thickness of fillet.

Pour vegetable mixture over fish and serve.

Christine's Continental Christmas Cake is a Treat

Ingredients

1 packet candied peel

1 packet green glacé cherries

1 packet red glacé cherries

1 cup raisins

½ cup pitted prunes, chopped

½ cup dried apricots, chopped

½ cup dates

½ cup preserved ginger

¾ cup mixture of nuts, chopped (brazil, walnuts, almonds — ¼ cup of each)

1 cup flour

½ tsp baking powder

2 eggs

1 tsp pure vanilla essence

¼ cup brandy, optional

Preheat oven to 135°C.

Mix fruit, ginger and nuts in a large bowl. Add sifted flour and baking powder and mix well.

Beat eggs with vanilla essence and stir in brandy if desired.

Slowly beat egg mixture into dry ingredients.

Press into lined cake tin.

Cover top with layer of greaseproof paper to prevent burning.

Bake 2 hours at 140°C. Turn oven off and leave cake inside to cool slowly.

Store in sealed container in fridge — will last for months.

Protein Shake

Serves 1

Consider this shake your daily protection against arthritis. I have one at 10 am and another at around 4 pm.

Ingredients

300ml water (distilled)

30g ion-exchange whey protein concentrate

1 tbsp flaxseed oil

1 tbsp organic pumpkin seeds

1 tbsp whole almonds

1 cup fresh fruit or frozen blueberries

1 banana

Blend ingredients at high speed. Drink immediately.

7. Up and running

Ready ...

Exercise is like meditation, food preparation and goal setting — if you don't think you have time to do them, then it's even more important that you think bigger and make that time. The stressed, overcommitted person needs the decluttering of meditation; the person who is too busy to make long-term plans will never get out of the sand dunes; and the person who eats fast food or microwaved meals is slowly being poisoned, which is no way to save time.

Similarly, if you get fit, not only will you achieve more in the time you have available, you will have many more years in which to enjoy bigger goals.

Our bodies are made to be used. Just like a fine instrument, they need constant retuning and will last longer the more attention we give them. It is important when exercising to push to constantly improve.

At the minimum I recommend some form of cardio activity — such as brisk walking — and strength training.

The media transmit many messages to the effect that all one needs to do is 20 minutes' walking, three times a week, to maintain fitness. That is certainly better than nothing, but it is not going to keep you in anything like your potential peak condition.

To be effective, exercise has to be done at an

> A healthy body is a guest chamber for the soul; a sick body is a prison.
>
> Sir Francis Bacon

elevated heart rate. The optimum rate varies according to age, but you can find out yours from your doctor or trainer.

I exercise regularly and for extended periods. I have got a lot of benefit from brisk walking for at least an hour in the fresh air. This is not always possible in our cities, but you can usually find a park where the calming influence of nature will go to work while you work up a sweat.

A good rule of thumb for working out: if you can talk comfortably to a companion while exercising, then you're not exercising hard enough.

The most useful piece of equipment you can have is a personal trainer. A qualified trainer can make a huge difference to how effectively you exercise. They can tailor routines that meet your specific needs — playing to your strengths and working on your weaknesses. That will prevent injury.

You won't have any problem with motivation for exercise because fitness is simply part of you achieving your 30-year goal. However, the trainer will get better results for you by psychologically pushing you to work that little bit harder at each session. That means that at the next session you are building from a higher baseline.

Because our bodies take the path of least resistance, any exercise programme soon turns into a routine. You need to change your programme every six to eight weeks to get the best results.

Get set: How to make the most of a weights programme

Get a clearance from your doctor before joining a gym.

Do not try to learn on your own.

Exercise four days a week.

Get a personal trainer to give you a specific programme and prevent injury by showing you how to perform exercises properly.

Warm up first until you are sweating (rowing is best).

Stretch between sets.

Change your workout every six to eight weeks, as variation increases strength and well-being.

Drink a litre of water during each workout.

Breathe: take a deep breath in and exhale while lifting until fully exhaled at the top of a lift. Take another full breath and exhale while lowering the weight.

Do not exercise for more than 45 minutes.

An excellent book to get started is the *Colgan Power Program*. This companion book allows you to record your weight training on charts and comes with a full description and photographic guide to each exercise.

Above all, take it easy and start slowly with weights you can handle in comfort; otherwise you will be sore and stiff as a board and never go again.

8. It's not brain surgery — if you act now

I came to know Dr Michael Colgan when he lived in New Zealand. He is regarded as one of the world's experts on the brain and anti-ageing. The following is from my many conversations with him on his research and from the book he has written, *Save Your Brain*, available from www.colganinstitute.com.

Prior to 1997 it was believed that you are born with brain cells that decline as you age. However, this all changed when the Salk Institute of California, USA, showed that new cells were being formed every day. So to prevent further damage to your brain we can take measures to not only prevent mental decline, but to put back the clock and bring our necktop computer up to its full working capacity.

A lot of brain damage and gradual decline is due to pollutants. I remember my father covering the vegetables in our garden with 'derris dust' (rotenone) to kill the caterpillars. There was lead in paint, lead in petrol, lead in water pipes, if a thermometer broke we used to play with the mercury, DDT fly sprays, mercury dental fillings, polluted drinking water, cigarette smoke, toxic weed sprays . . . the list goes on and on. All those pollutants affect the quality of your brain's performance and lead to eventual loss of memory and the possible threat of dementia, stroke, Alzheimer's or Parkinson's disease.

Many of the above substances are now banned but another group have taken their place, such as BPA bisphenyl-A used in the making of plastic, as a coating on metal cans to protect the metal from the food content, as a plastic in food and water bottles, refrigerator shelving, microwave ovens and eating utensils, to name a few. These are carcinogenic. Also toxins in the air are almost impossible to avoid in large cities. New Zealand is one of the few countries in the world that allows pesticides to be freely sprayed from the air.

So the key to keeping your necktop computer in tip-top shape is to take preventative measures now to stop brain ageing. Many of the supplements and pharmaceutical drugs used to treat dementia, Parkinson's disease, Alzheimer's disease, Huntington's disease, etc., if taken in small doses from mid-age can protect you from these brain diseases.

See your anti-ageing physician or contact the Colgan Institute for more details — www.colganinstitute.com

9. Speaking of manners

My mother Billie was a wonderful cook. All meals were prepared at home and eaten sitting at the dining table, with serviettes and nicely laid settings. The table was covered in a crisp, ironed and starched white linen tablecloth.

From the moment I could hold a knife and fork, I was taught how to do so properly along with other basic table manners. I knew which side to put my serviette on, how to half unfold it and place it over my knees. I knew how to leave the knife and fork on my plate when I had finished eating (lined up parallel in the centre of the plate).

There were other rules of etiquette drummed into me, too, from an early age — simple things like standing up when a guest enters the room, not sitting at the table until all the women were seated. As I grew older I learnt how to decant a wine over a candle on the rare occasion a red wine was opened in our house. Because restaurants were few in number, eating out was a rarely exercised option, and dinner was the hub of family life and a chance for us to learn about food, wine and etiquette.

> There were rules of etiquette drummed into me from an early age — **simple things like standing up when a guest enters the room.**

Today even when people eat at home, it is likely to be in front of the television or in separate rooms, instead of as a group sharing a meal and each other's company.

Good manners make life more agreeable for everyone.

Many of these meals will not even have been cooked at home. They will have come from a supermarket, bought frozen and heated up in a microwave.

We lose a lot in our race to do things more quickly and easily. Instant gratification seems to be accepted in all areas of life — from the evening meal to the job that you chuck in because it wasn't quite the walk in the park you expected it to be. When the going gets tough, the not-so-tough get going out the door.

My recollections may sound quaint now but believe me it made life a lot more pleasant. Good manners make life more agreeable for everyone. Nowadays, they also help you gain a winning edge in all areas of life because they are so rarely encountered. Anyone who consistently displays good manners will stand out as a cut above the rest. People with noticeably poor manners, on the other hand, carry a handicap around with them constantly.

There have been times when I have felt embarrassed for some of my top people because they were unaware of correct manners. I've had to teach them myself. One was very egalitarian: when he met someone, it didn't matter who they were, he said, 'Gidday', and if he happened to be sitting down that is how he stayed. He never stood up to meet anyone.

He also held his food with his fork as if he was worried it would run off the plate, and hacked at it with his knife like an apprentice butcher with a lazy eye. Such behaviour doesn't directly affect how someone does their job, but it does directly affect how other people perceive them — negatively.

And these days only someone like me is going to bother correcting them. Otherwise there's just a cycle of poorly mannered people being imitated by others and constantly lowering standards of behaviour. If you're lucky these days, you might see a parent telling a kid not to talk with his mouth full but that's about as far as it goes.

Many if not all of our rules and instructions vary between cultures. For instance, I'm never sure if I'm holding chopsticks correctly. But that doesn't mean you give up. It means you try to educate yourself so you will do things well out of respect for the people you are with.

Many books have been written about manners and among the most useful are those by 'Miss Manners', the pen-name of Judith Martin, which are thoughtful and up to date. As society changes, we need to develope etiquette for new situations. Manners have also come fully into the twenty-first century: www.emilypost.com is the website of the Emily Post Institute, which that great expert on etiquette founded in 1946. Her descendants are still involved with the institute and the website has a huge amount of good advice on manners for all occasions.

It's not what you do that is important. It is the fact that you bothered to do it. Good manners are about more than how you hold a knife and fork. They are about an attitude to other people and a philosophy of life that is humane and respectful.

That said, there are some underlying principles behind all good manners.

Three golden rules

1 Respect	You acknowledge that the other person deserves to be treated as you would like to be treated.
2 Empathy	Try to observe how other people are feeling, mirror their mood and act accordingly.
3 Selflessness	Put others first. Good manners are often made up of small sacrifices.

10 commandments

Building on those three golden rules are 10 commandments — rules of etiquette that are acceptable everywhere. They apply broadly to everything from eating out to visiting someone's home to taking a business meeting.

1 Say please when you ask for something and thank you when you receive it.

2 Don't interrupt. Wait your turn to speak.

3 Wait and take your turn in all other areas too.

4 Show interest in what other people are saying. Don't just wait impatiently for them to finish so you can start talking. Listen!

5 Be punctual. And if you're early, wait until the agreed time before letting your arrival be known.

6 Don't take or make phone calls or texts during meetings, conversations or in restaurants.

7 Always stand up and shake hands when meeting someone. Do the same when they or you leave.

8 Clean up after yourself. Leave spaces as you found them.

9 Open doors for others and stand back to let them go through — cars, offices, homes — this applies everywhere.

10 Respect other people's differences and cultures even if you are not sure why they do what they do.

Hello

Hello

10. Manners of speaking

You can have all your goals set, your necktop computer perfectly programmed and your winning edge calculated exactly — in fact, you can have everything right — and ruin it all by speaking unclearly. I see this in the shops when very talented people fail on the floor because the customer can't hear them properly or can't understand what they are saying.

The ability to speak clearly and engagingly to one person or a thousand when you have a message to share is crucial to thinking bigger. The world is full of people who mumble and struggle to be understood. If that's who you want to be, you will have plenty of competition. Or you can step outside the pack and choose to be an effective and powerful public speaker.

Because everybody has to sell themselves, everybody should have some experience of public speaking. Even if it's only at a wedding or a twenty-first birthday party or a funeral, chances are you are going to have to talk to a large group sooner or later. How sad not to be able to perform your duty at such a function because you were too nervous about your ability as a speaker.

I wrote earlier about how fear of public speaking is usually an example of a badly programmed necktop computer. You can do courses or join groups like Toastmasters. Some are more practical or will appeal more than others. At a Dale Carnegie course, for example, if you don't speak passionately enough, the rest of the class hits you with rolled-up newspapers. I'm not sure that is absolutely necessary, but it's probably less humiliating than seeing people walk out of a room while you're making a hash of delivering a speech.

People regard me as an accomplished speaker, and it is true that

I enjoy it very much now, but it's a miracle I have ended up with that reputation. I used to be terrified at the thought of speaking in public. It started when I had to speak to a few staff in the shop. Then I had to give my first proper speech to about 450 people and I was terrified about that. But once you've got the hang of it, there's actually no difference whether you're speaking to one person or a million and it's a great feeling when you do. If everybody did some form of public speaking it would give a real boost to their confidence and self-esteem.

I was lucky early on to find Dale Carnegie's book on the subject, which has brilliant advice. He reminds you to do things like varying your rate of delivery — speed up and slow down. Variety is crucial. Even pauses and silence have their part to play if you know how to deploy them. We have all heard the speaker whose pitch and rhythm never vary — it's like going to a concert and listening to a violinist playing just one note.

I know prosperous people who have made a success of things without being able to speak well. One I can think of is hugely successful, but when he talks to you, you have to strain to make out what he's mumbling. That's a perfect example of not thinking bigger. He doesn't believe he needs to fix anything because he has done well. But if he was thinking bigger and had a more ambitious goal, he would realise that addressing that one aspect would open up new opportunities. How much more effective would he have been if he didn't mumble?

'**Michael** Hill jeweller', 'Michael **Hill** jeweller', 'Michael Hill **jeweller**'

One of the best things you can do to improve as a speaker is record your own voice and listen to it on playback. Most people are shocked at how different they sound, but that's what the people they talk to hear all the time. Hearing yourself in this way makes it easiest to identify flaws and mend them. You may speak too fast; you may get breathless; something that sounds coherent and sensible in your head may be garbled rubbish by the time it gets to your mouth. The recording will let you know.

I found this out by accident when I began doing my own adverts. You put earphones on and you hear your own voice. I was also able to work out words that I didn't pronounce quite clearly and practise them until they were right.

The other impediment to good speech is our old foe, fear, especially for sales staff whose necktop computer is cluttered with negative messages.

Staff can get nervous and outside their comfort zones when they start making big sales. They might think they have done well to sell a one-carat diamond at $6000, but suddenly someone comes in who wants to see a $20,000 ring. The salesperson seizes up and one of two things happens to their speech: they may start speaking twice as fast as they normally would soeverythingisajumble. Their neck tightens up and the voice becomes higher pitched. Or they become quieter and quieter till no one can hear a word.

Well, if you can't be heard you're not going to get past step one. But the three-metre rule soon fixes that.

Take three paces

In selling we use a practice technique called the three-metre test. First the person says something like, 'This is an interesting ring with a 58-facet brilliant cut diamond', up close. Then we get the person to step back one metre and repeat the message so that it is still as loud and clear as it was up close. We repeat this at two metres and three metres. It's the three-metre distance that generally needs to be used. This is such a simple thing, yet people who have been struggling find when they use it their sales go through the roof. They exude confidence and belief in what they are saying.

Training in how to speak well is now an essential part of the training when people join our company.

Speak up, I can't see you

Gesture is also crucial. When you do public speaking, you have to get away from the rostrum to get great results. It's quite difficult. You're behind this safety shield, where you can have all your notes and you've got your microphone — and all people can see is your little head. That's no good. You have to make yourself step out from behind it. Then you have to leave it completely and work with a lapel mike and no props. I found that difficult to start with, but it makes for a powerful presentation because there is absolutely nothing between you and the audience.

I found it very hard to be animated at first. I needed to warm up like you would before a workout. I found moving my body on stage difficult. I was self-conscious. Now I've relaxed into my own style, which I think everybody has if they can trust themselves and reprogramme the necktop computer for it.

People often don't know what to do with their hands when they finally come out from behind the lectern. They can hold on to it when they're there, but when they are exposed their hands can look awkward. After a while it becomes instinctive. I tend to wave mine about a bit and gesture a lot because I have been influenced by American speakers.

I don't recommend reading a written speech, nor do I recommend memorising a speech. That's the worst option of all as it sounds unemotional.

The best choice is to make bullet points. I used to do that and then write screeds of stuff under the bullet points, which defeated the purpose. After a while, too, you don't even consult your bullet points any more. They are there to fall back on in an emergency, but once you've got the flow going then what comes out will be more natural, less forced and more interesting than anything you might have in your notes.

It's also important to engage your audience. Make eye contact with individuals — this draws them towards you.

Visualisation is a great technique for successful public speaking. You can go through the whole thing in your mind and see yourself doing it perfectly. The more times you do this the better. You can practise the fully relaxed visualisation or you can do it when you're out for a run or walking the dog.

The power of one

I don't use PowerPoint for public speaking. In fact I try to avoid it whenever possible. Fortunately I grew up at a time when we didn't have aids like that to fall back on. We had to communicate using our voices, eyes and bodies.

Visual aids can be useful in certain circumstances but for speaking to people directly they are a distraction. I have lost count of how many times I have sat through a presentation where a speaker on stage merely reads out what is being projected on a screen behind him.

One of the components in that interaction isn't necessary.

Let me just finish by saying
1 Practise — try your speech out on a willing partner or colleague if you can. This will let you gauge what the most effective parts are.
2 Smile.
3 Know your audience. Have an ideal listener — real or imaginary — in your mind and tailor everything you say to them.
4 Always check out the venue before you speak.
5 Try and arrange the seating as close as possible to where you will give your address. This way you will be able to remain attached to your audience while presenting.
6 Check out the sound systems and have new batteries fitted to the lapel mike.
7 Move around and see that there are no areas where your speech is distorted through electrical interference.
8 Have a glass of water handy.

9 Vary the tone of your voice.

10 Pause for up to four seconds between points.

11 Move around on stage.

12 Slow down and speed up your delivery.

13 Relax and trust yourself.

14 Be humble.

15 Make eye contact.

16 Look happy, look sad.

17 Be emotional.

18 The most important parts of the speech are the beginning and ending, so make these powerful.

19 Dress smartly. This shows people you respect them, so they are likelier to respect you.

20 Be funny by all means. But don't just try to be funny. See rule one above to find out whether or not you will get that laugh. If not, don't try.

21 Where possible — if the group size allows it — invite questions. Don't let the questions get in the way of what you are there to say, and don't let that one annoying questioner hog the floor. But do remember that a conversation can be much more effective communication than a sermon.

22 Invite feedback and take it seriously.

Further reading

The Art of Public Speaking by Dale Carnegie, available free online at manybooks.net

11. Take it on the nose

I'm surprised at how often a talented person who has done a great job of making himself or herself presentable undoes all their hard work by having awful breath.

For a customer who might have been thinking about making a purchase, the deal ends then and there. Who is going to buy an item as full of symbolic significance as a diamond ring — something that is designed to last forever — if they know that every time they look at it, they are going to be reminded of the sales assistant's halitosis and that terrible odour?

This is no exaggeration by the way — scientists have discovered that the sense of smell is closely associated with the part of the brain that deals with emotional memories. That is why odours are such powerful triggers for memories of especially significant experiences.

Most bad breath comes from deep down inside your body. Fortunately there are several things that can be done about it, starting at the top. Obviously it is essential to clean your teeth regularly and, even more importantly, floss to get rid of those bits of food that linger around until they decay and start to give off a rotting odour.

Use a tongue scraper, which has become part of my routine. I use it first thing in the morning when I wake up. A quick scrape and it is amazing how much gunk that has accumulated on your tongue comes off. It's also an interesting experiment to wipe the gunk off the scraper and onto the basin. If you don't wash it away immediately, it becomes almost rock hard and you have to scrub vigorously to get it off later. I can only imagine what it does to your system if it is left in there.

If your breath is still bad, then you have to attack the problem at source — that could mean acidophilus yoghurt, which will get down into your gut and eat up the bacteria causing bad breath.

Stained teeth can affect your appearance and ability to sell yourself. As always, it's the little things that count. Visit a hygienist, who will polish your teeth, floss and check for cavities, every six months. I have heard of a US celebrity who drinks coffee through a straw because he doesn't want to risk it discolouring his teeth. I wouldn't go that far, but a bonus of all the breath-protection strategies is that they are going to help your teeth stay whiter by keeping your mouth cleaner.

Finally, apart from the social and commercial disadvantages of bad breath, if someone has that much going wrong in their digestive system, it's going to be affecting their thinking and performance in other areas so should also be dealt with for that reason.

See *Toughen Up*, pages 69-70.

12. Family values

Pair shaped

Although this is a book about realising individual potential, life is not meant to be lived alone, and unless we treat our personal relationships with as much respect and care as we can, then that ultimate goal of happiness is going to elude us.

If two people share the same 30-year goal, then their lives together will be a lot easier. If they have very different goals, there is a high chance their relationship won't survive. The sooner they discover whether or not their goals match, the better. Most people find out before they commit to a long-term relationship.

In our day, people used to jump into marriage too early, which can create its own problems. We married later — Christine was 25 and I was 26 when we got married. We didn't have any kids for four years until she was 29, which was considered quite late back then. Christine wanted to go on teaching and we wanted to get more established. If we had started a family straight away, then it would have been difficult to get ahead.

I have been lucky in that Christine came to share my goal, although I have to acknowledge she sacrificed some of her own goals, or at least postponed them, along the way. She would have liked to put more time into her art, which is her great passion and her great talent.

On balance she decided that she would be happier making the choices we did, but it definitely required some adjusting. Now she is able to put a lot of effort into her art and I am immensely proud of what she produces. She is also creating a wonderful range of signature jewellery for us. But I know there were times in the past when she felt the effort wasn't worth it. There were initial hardships and discomfort that we had to work through. 'Why are we bothering doing this?' she asked more than once as my goals grew bigger.

It helped us a lot that we were brought up in such a beautiful place as northern New Zealand, which gave us such a balanced lifestyle. When Christine and I were children, and as young parents ourselves, we used to have a real family life. The evening meal was the thing. Everyone sat down together to eat. Everything focused around families spending time together. Home entertainment systems meant a piano or violin, or some board games or a record player.

We have to bring back some of the good old-fashioned values that this generation seems to be moving away from. Make meal time an important event. Eat at home, cook your own food from local produce and engage the family in the process. Have children lay the table correctly, watch their manners, clean up and do the dishes afterwards. The television is off. The mobiles and phone are off. Make an affair of these occasions and notice what it does for communication within the family.

Too often today the meals are heated-up packets and the entertainment is electronic and online. Children text with one hand while shovelling down food with the other, and Dad is having his meal in front of the TV.

We need to present ourselves in relationships in the best possible light. In a way, asking a girl out is like applying for a job. We are working hard to make her think we are the right candidate for this very special opportunity she has available.

We find out the things she is interested in and learn about them so we can share the interest with her. And we should try to never lose those values that attracted us to each other — so we groom, we keep ourselves healthy, we dress nicely, and we respect each other. Just because you are married, doesn't mean you drop any of the little things that drew you together.

Structure is important; routine is important. Just as for people in business, children in families need to know where they fit. Structure is very much a Hill family characteristic. We respect family values and are organised in the things we do. All the basic things are done in a way that helps us get to our goals.

No human can cope with too large a range of activities. In the attempt to work full time and run a household and have a family, something will have to give unless the couple share everything and complement each other, or negotiate roles and responsibilities so that everything gets done and no one gets done over.

Again, I was lucky because Michael Hill Jeweller was a partnership from the start. Without Christine it wouldn't have happened. I aimed high but she kept my feet on the ground. I probably would have floated away without her to provide the necessary balance.

Golden — and diamond — rules

Buy her a diamond ring and tell her you love her all over again.

Always show respect for your partner.

Never take them for granted.

Try always to look your best.

Bring the romance back into your life and look back at what attracted you in the first place.

Laugh together like you used to do.

When did you last give your partner a bunch of flowers or a simple card saying, 'I love you' and a kiss with a thank you?

Take another look at yourself in the mirror naked. Do you think you still look attractive? If not, what are you going to do about it? It may be time to start the diet and exercise programme, get a new haircut and some smarter clothes, and reset your goals together.

What did you use to do outdoors together that attracted you to each other? If you no longer do things together, it may be a good idea to change this.

Parent traps

Just as a parent needs to be like a good boss and not dictate to children but delegate, so they also need to get out on the 'shop floor'. They need to get alongside their kids and spend time with them to show that they are willing to be part of the same process.

But just as you stuff up if you get too close to staff and try to be friends instead of colleagues, you will have the same problem if you try to be 'one of the kids'. At the same time as you are very close, you need to respect your own positions — parents are parents and kids are kids. A lot of parents these days are more like big versions of their own kids. They can't draw that line and create the discipline and boundaries that young people need to help them grow into responsible adults.

Even grandparents these days are often too busy filling up their lives with activities to play a part in their families. When our children were small we were often away on business, sometimes for weeks. Christine's parents were only too happy to have them and grandparents' values are often a great influence on children's lives. My children have wonderful memories and have learned a lot from spending time with their grandparents. That is a very old-fashioned way of being — it's not about having a modern, fast-paced life. A hundred or more years ago, several generations of a family lived together so that if one set of parents couldn't be around, the grandparents were on the spot to take up the slack. I'm sure it was very healthy for children to be exposed to a different generation to such an extent at such a young age.

Now, I am very proud that both our children and their families live on our property at The Hills, in their own homes.

I think we have the balance right.

It's wonderful that Emma works in the business. It's also wonderful that Mark has found his bliss and a lot of success as a sculptor. He is very much his own man, very laid back and very fulfilled. But no one would ever mistake him for me.

He worked in our office in Australia for a while and once we realised he was not a nine-to-five man who would be happy going to work in a suit, we didn't try to fit him into a slot. When he didn't want to stay in the business any more, that was fine. Emma, on the other hand, is fanatical about it.

Balance

Now we have developed our work skills and our life skills, it's time to think **BIGGER** and bring them together by applying some laws of balance and natural order.

1. Hidden depths —
how meditation changed my life and my business

When I discovered the amazing power of transcendental meditation (TM), I had the missing key to unlocking the door to my goals. It has enabled me to clear my mind of all distractions and unlocked a wellspring of creativity.

Yes, this is the same transcendental meditation taught by the Maharishi Mahesh Yogi, whose most famous followers included the Beatles. The knowledge of it has been handed down from initiate to initiate and its roots lie many centuries back in ancient Indian ayurvedic teachings.

If you have any aversion to new-age, airy-fairy ideas then this is the one section of this book you must read because the basic practice of TM is none of those things. I could have included this part of the book in the Work section or the Life section. I guess that's why it's ended up in the section on Balance — because it is equally relevant to both areas.

Remember back at the beginning of this book when you started to think about goals and how to deprogramme the necktop computer to get rid of negative self-talk? Well, meditation is the simplest and most effective way to do that. It can be as good as a week-long business seminar or a year-long therapy course. Simply: meditation empties your mind so it can do its stuff.

The brain is one of the few things in creation that works at 100 per cent capacity when it is idle. A brain that is free and devoid of all thought is capable of running, and it doesn't need you to interfere with it. Leave it to get on with the job.

TM is practised twice a day for 20 minutes each time. It's not a big time commitment and it's an effortless process. You don't have to do special exercises. Basically, if you can sit down and be quiet, you can do TM.

For some people 20 minutes twice a day is a big amount of free time to find. They are on the go from the moment they get up, with kids to get to school, then work, then dinner to prepare. Naturally, these are the people who need to practise TM most of all.

No one is indispensable. Take a glass full of water, put your finger in the water and take it out again. That's how much difference you make if you disappear suddenly. Any enterprise should be able to survive without someone for 20 minutes.

If you have a partner, the two of you need to work out how to free up some time. Be inventive: you can do TM in the car when you get home from work before going inside the house. You can do TM while waiting for an appointment. Or travelling by aeroplane — you can tune out wherever you are!

In TM we transcend the everyday and connect with our inner self. By repeating a mantra, we experience several effects without consciously willing them to happen. One is that our self-talk goes away and our mind is left open. I believe it connects us with all our ancestors — as many 'greats' before grandparents as you care to imagine — back to the beginning of time. It unlocks the memory that is imprinted in our DNA and gives us all the inherited characteristics that evolved over the years. To be able to connect with that, even in some small way, is tremendously energising. It's an amazing feeling when you get to this state. You do feel like you're part of everything else in the universe.

Occasionally you reach a point of total stillness — not always, but occasionally. Sometimes your mind rambles a lot but other times, suddenly, everything seems to go still. Sometimes you've done it for 20 minutes and it feels like it has only been two minutes. At other times, two minutes can seem like 20. There is no right or wrong or good or bad about what you feel when you are doing it.

I know Emma found it very useful when she was doing her Bachelor of Commerce and MBA, and still does now she has the twins, Chloe and Jacob. Christine also talks about how helpful she has found it. There have been times when she has had a problem and been wondering what to do about it. Then, after meditation, although not aware she has been thinking about the problem, she comes out knowing just what to do about it. That's another very common experience.

Some people experience a strong emotional effect. One person in the group when I was learning said she was just crying inside during the whole thing, although there were no tears on the surface. She came out of the meditation and was really freaked out. She said if that was going to happen every time she didn't want to do it again. The teacher explained that it might, but she was not to worry because it was just the meditation getting rid of all the stress and tension she had bottled up.

When you have an experience like that it can be scary and off-putting. But every meditation experience is different. It is as though the brain decides to get out of the experience just what it needs at that time.

Meditation is a rewarding practice even when things are going well. It's not just for the bad times. That said, if one is getting stressed or bogged down and everything is coming at you at once; if the phone keeps ringing or there's an

In transcendental meditation we experience **pure awareness.**

accident happened and someone's cut their finger and needs you to see to them while you're supposed to be somewhere else and you are in a whirl ... STOP.

Just a few minutes of meditation can make all the difference. Suddenly all that self-chatter that is just confusing and stressing you will be cleared away. Your priorities will make themselves apparent. It can be a quick fix as well as a long-term one.

Looked at dispassionately from the businessperson's point of view, TM will help as far as reaching our 30-year goal or doubling our incomes. The reason is very simple and practical: it helps because it is a simple process for freeing up our thoughts, clearing out some space for new ideas that are going to invigorate our thinking.

> **TM is a simple process for freeing up our thoughts, clearing out some space for new ideas.**

I should emphasise that TM is the answer to successfully achieving balance. It's a way of clearing things up so we can get on with looking for the answer. When you're down at the bottom of the dune, trapped in the sand, it will blow all the sand away and you will be able to see how to climb out of the hole.

There are also amazing health benefits. The immune system is boosted. High blood pressure should become a thing of the past. If you're more interested in your outside appearance than your internal health, removing that stress can take years off. And if you are one of those people who believe that stress plays a role in the formation and progress of cancer, then anything that reduces stress will have obvious benefits.

When I came to TM — which was through some friends who were very serious practitioners — I was already on my way to ending negative self-talk. I had formulated my goals. But TM made the process so much easier. I firmly believe that if TM hadn't found me at the right time, I may not have reached my goals. It has removed the unnecessary self-talk that would have built up stress and tension.

I mentioned earlier in this book that I welcomed change. A corollary of that is a willingness to try something different. I'll try anything once. And something that works as well as TM has for me I will practise again and again.

Christine and I learnt it together. When we were first introduced to it, it had an instant effect. It's good for couples to do it together because then each understands what is happening to the other. It's unsettling for one half of a couple if the other has to disappear and sit still for 20 minutes twice a day.

When we started Michael Hill Jeweller, I was disappointed that I failed to introduce TM across my company. I got instructors to come to our head office and teach my top people but my CEO at the time didn't believe in it. Because of one person not getting with the programme, the whole process didn't flow naturally. That attitude got passed down the line and I couldn't make it work.

However, there are companies where TM is practised at the beginning and end of the day, and they report much better relations among workers and between workers and management. They also show greater productivity.

Transcendental meditation needs to be taught by a trained instructor for several reasons, including to make sure you follow correct practice and to adjust your expectations so that they are realistic. An experienced TM trainer will also help you find a mantra of words that best suit your body type.

TM is practised in a comfortable upright position, preferably in a quiet place. But if there's noise in the background you can't control, just do the meditation anyway.

It is critical to get the right mantra, so TM should not be practised without one. You begin slowly by saying the word to yourself. If your word was 'mantra', for instance, you think the word without saying it aloud.

Your mind will wander; you will think of other things, perhaps even including some doubt about why you are doing this. When your attention strays, gently but firmly go back to mentally saying your password: 'Mantra, mantra, mantra.'

Practise, and, I must emphasise, practise effortlessly. You can't *try* to meditate. It has to be a non-judgemental and effortless process. The self-talk and chatter become less. The little voices begin to stop pestering you, and you start to experience true quietness, free of all self-talk. After the 20 minutes is up you will have an unbelievably clear head.

It is as though you have inserted a disc cleaner into your computer to erase all the bad viruses that slow down the speed and affect the time it takes to send and receive messages. Until I practised TM I had never experienced the quietness required to free up space in my necktop computer to set our future direction.

Clean up the programme

There are many other methods of meditation, like concentration on the in and out breath. There is even a walking meditation. I recommend the book *The Three-Minute Meditator,* by David Harp and Nina Smiley (see page 55). David is a passionate advocate of this three-minute meditation technique. His breath counting technique may be an alternative for you. I like it. You simply count your breaths — concentrate on them and count: 'Inhale ... Exhale ... 1, Inhale ... Exhale ... 2, Inhale ... Exhale ... 3, Inhale ... Exhale ... 4, then repeat from 1 again' and so on. You can do this while performing any other action, anywhere at any time.

For more information see www.tm.org.nz

2. Free time is the most precious time

I have huge amounts of free time. It's one of the paradoxical secrets to thinking bigger. It's surprising how few people do have free time, but it is something that seems to be created as a result of meditation. With the mind clear of clutter, we stop wasting time on non-essential, repetitive thought patterns.

There are two types of free time, which are like opposite swings of the pendulum. One is the free time that takes you effortlessly towards your goal and is in itself a valuable creative activity. The other is time in which you have chosen to do nothing. Maybe you have retired or lost interest in the future. I cannot imagine what that would be like.

The first kind of free time is the antidote to a heavy workload. You could be extremely busy, running a big business and turning into an absolute stress ball. People might be coming at you from all directions, wanting all sorts of things. In a case like this, the stress is self-induced. The necktop computer has to work double time. It feels like it's about to explode because you've got so many things going on in there.

People in this position have only themselves to blame. We had a senior staff member who was a genius in many ways, but he filled up his time with unnecessary tasks. His job was to choose people to manage his department. But he never could find the perfect person to replace himself with. We had highly qualified people applying from all over the world but no one was quite right for him.

We realised eventually that the reason he never chose anyone was because he could not stand the idea of sharing what he saw as his power and authority. He would work ridiculous hours. When everyone else had gone home by 6 pm — which they should —

he would stay later and then take work home. We knew from the computers that he was often doing work at 4 am. We tried to get him to work fewer hours, but I don't think he had ever heard the word 'balance'.

When he and his wife were expecting a baby he arranged for her to have a caesarean and scheduled it so that he would still be able to keep his normal work appointments around that time.

He's gone over to one of our competitors now. I hope for his sake they will be happier about him working around the clock than I could be. It was a great example to me of how stupid smart people can be. He had the capacity to do anything. He was extraordinarily bright. But he had that one enormous weakness — he couldn't control his time. He never learnt to trust people, to train people and to delegate.

At the root of this was his core problem — he was worried about having free time. This is not uncommon. Some people are scared to be alone in their own heads. But that is the most creative space in the world.

On the other hand, I have a friend here in Queenstown who owns a lot of buildings in town as well as substantial property overseas. He is wealthy but everything is under the radar, quietly working away on his behalf. He never seems to be too busy. As a result, his net worth would be 50 times what my former employee will ever have.

His secret? He has freed up his time sufficiently to be able to think of the big picture. Until we can free ourselves up in this way, we can never take that step back to see things in context or take the time to visualise how we want things to be. We spend all our time running to stay in one place.

When we free ourselves up from huge working days,

> Free time lets us step back to see things in perspective and visualise the way forward.

we go faster, not slower. We are just culling unnecessary distractions to allow us to concentrate.

However, it's easy to cross a very fine line and cull so much that we are effectively comatose. I think many creative ideas come when we are doing some kind of activity that is unconnected — on the golf course perhaps, or while cooking. A lot of my creative ideas come when I am out on the shop floor with the team on a busy day.

The other mistake people make with free time is that they postpone it indefinitely. They think they need to get everything done before they can have free time: 'Once I've got all this finished, I'll sit down and have some time to myself.'

Of course, if you think like that, you will never have free time because new things will constantly come along and demand to be done. You have to make yourself stop and stay still. The things will get done in their own time, not your time.

One of my board members has mastered this. You can never call him before 11.30 am. He will not answer the phone until that hour. He has worked out that the morning is his best time and he needs to keep it free of other people's distractions. No emails. No phone calls. Everybody has a cycle of productivity. We need to know when ours is.

> # Free up your **most productive time** to nail the **important task**.

Turn off the noise

Most people are fresher in the morning, but not everyone is. Once you have discovered your 100 per cent time, make sure you make the most of it. Schedule the priority for the day to be performed in that part of your cycle.

Distractions are constantly put in our way to eat up our free time. Perhaps the worst, although important, is the computer and mobile phone. When we are involved in some task and hear it go ping, it is very hard not to stop what we are involved in and check. It takes discipline not to be distracted.

It might be something important but it hardly ever is. And it is almost never something that could not wait until we had finished what we were doing.

The computer and mobile phone are meant to be aids, but because they distract us from our focus and eat up our free time, they actually add to our stress. So turn them off.

3. Let go and hold on

Closely related to the concept of free time and how it enables us to keep balance in our life is the notion of letting go in order to hold on to things. To do this, we need to learn to trust and make the most of our intuition.

We can programme our necktop computer to a large extent, but there is also a great deal going on in our subconscious that we need to be aware of. We all seem to have an inbuilt ability to sense things. I know I can walk past one of my shops and know whether it's going all right or not just from a glance. And I think even customers can sense when something's in sync or not. We have all had the experience of going into a shop or a cafe and feeling things aren't quite right and turning on our heels to go straight back out again.

In the case of my shops I don't need to consciously determine what needs attention. The 'brain beneath my brain' notices and my conscious brain identifies the whole process as 'intuition'.

We all have an inbuilt ability to sense things.

So there is every reason to take advantage of what our intuition tells us. It can be a great time saver.

The same thing happens when we meet people for the first time. Our first impression is the one that will stay with us and it is nearly always right. Again I think this has a perfectly sound scientific basis. Over the years we have met many people. Some we have liked and some we have disliked. Subconsciously our brain has kept a record of the common characteristics of the people we liked and of those we disliked. It automatically runs a check on new people and matches them up with those records. This is what we call our first impression.

I like decisions at Michael Hill Jeweller to be made swiftly. Add up the pros and cons but make a quick decision. In retailing things move very quickly and if decisions are left undecided we may miss out altogether on a big opportunity. Trust your intuition or gut feeling and get on with the job. You're usually right!

In the future we will understand a lot more about the workings of intuition and the subconscious. Everyone has had the experience of thinking of someone, perhaps on the other side of the world, and then finding out something significant was happening to them at that very moment. At the moment this is beyond comprehension. But I do know that our abilities are greater than we realise.

Best of all, these are effortless skills. No one has to practise intuition. Just let go and let it do its work. It doesn't need any help from us. We can even prevent it from doing its job by concentrating too much on the power of the necktop computer. That needs to be programmed and then left to get on with it.

It's the same as how we can ruin the practice of meditation by 'trying' to meditate: 'I'm trying really hard to meditate.' Trying is the opposite of the effortless serenity that meditation brings. Once you try to do it, you're not doing it. Once you try to tap into your intuition, you lose your intuition. Let it go.

Take things easy and you get better results. Do it hard and your effort gets in the way of your goal. Unfortunately we have been brought up to believe success comes from hard work. In some senses that is true, but not always. People distort the idea of hard work and take it to mean that if they are not successful, the answer is to work harder. If they are still not successful despite working harder, they try to work harder still. Which result will come first: meltdown or burnout? The one thing they will not achieve is the success they crave.

> **No one has to practise intuition.** Let go and let it do its work. It doesn't need our help.

Instead of working harder, they should work less. They should at least start going to bed earlier and getting more sleep. That gives all our aspects — brain, hormones, creativity — time to renew themselves. They are the real determinants of how successful we will be.

You can almost guarantee, too, that a person who has not learnt the art of letting go has not understood that the ultimate goal is happiness.

4. The serious business of fun

We need fun in our lives. We can be reluctant to express that happiness is part of our ultimate goal, so fun can seem a little ...trivial.

On the contrary, it is vital.

Make time to enjoy doing things that bring you happiness. Not to have fun is to risk serious mental, emotional and ultimately physical consequences. Fun is crucial to balancing the various aspects of our life.

If you get too steeped in your goal and don't take breaks or let go so your intuition can do the steering, you're not going to be able to see anything balanced.

Everyone's idea of fun is slightly different. Christine likes

> **Fun is crucial** to balancing the various aspects of our life.

getting outside and back to nature. Fun for her is going for a walk or turning over some soil. Gardening is therapeutic fun for many people, whether it's getting your hands dirty or pruning trees and making a fire out of the leaves. Getting back to nature and the real world is calming and exhilarating at the same time. She also always says that

---

'By the time you get to a certain age, it is easy to become very good at fooling yourself about where your life is at, which is just as well, as otherwise you would self-destruct with loathing. Look at people as they get older — they get fat, they get lazy, they expect life to get easy.'

Escape to the Pole, by Kevin Biggar

---

when she uses her artistic ability she becomes a better person.

Take time in your busy schedule to take notice of the small pleasures in life: the effortless flight of a bird, the smell of newly mown grass, the smell of the ocean — these thoughts and feelings can stay in your mind's eye all day and help you sail through the day.

Always make sure you have time to indulge in your passion — maybe you love to tinker with old cars, create embroidery, walk in woods, play an instrument — you must never be too busy to do what you love and it will help you love what you do.

I am having a lot of fun pursuing my goal of 1000 stores.

5. The bank balance

One of the best things you can do with money, I found, is to give it away. I have been closely involved with Cure Kids, the children's health charity, New Zealand golf and the Michael Hill International Violin Competition, the latter of which has been a wonderful way to give money away to young musicians.

Money is also a useful yardstick of business success, although I have been much more interested in having a successful business than in getting money out of it.

> One of the best things you can do with money is **to give it away.**

But money is most definitely not a measure of a person's worth. I can go out to dinner with wealthy people who bore me witless. And I can go out to dinner with people who have no money but are very interesting, thought-provoking individuals. Best of all is not knowing, so you judge people completely on their merits.

Christine feels uncomfortable if people treat her differently when they realise 'who she is'. Even when we are in cities where we are not well known, she might have a piece of jewellery that shows evidence of some prosperity. Suddenly the waiter or shop assistant's attitude to her changes completely. It's superficial. And if she is not wearing the diamond she is not treated nearly so well, even though, of course, she is exactly the same person on each occasion.

For myself, I don't mind. I enjoy talking to anyone regardless. Now that we have a large yacht we are exposed to some very strange behaviour. The super-yacht world is a whole new level of one-up-manship and some of the people who own these boats are very

You can do without an awful lot **and still be happy.**

different from the people we mix with.

In the early days, my crew were concerned at us even wanting to talk to them as it is not uncommon for the crew to provide invisible service. Many super-yacht owners have cameras everywhere and all the crew have walkie-talkies. When the owner is approaching, the crew call ahead to each other to get out of the way, even if it means hiding in a broom cupboard. The owners seldom see the crew. They want it to seem as if they are on the boat alone, away from it all.

We are on first-name terms with the crew and we prefer to encourage open communication to build a stronger team by recognising improvements in performance. This way the crew know where they stand, are happier, give better results and stay with us longer. For me, invisible service would mean invisible results.

Treat everyone you meet as equals. Everyone is important but no one is very important!

6. The art of living

The arts have played a big part in my life. I would have liked them to play a bigger part, but it was not to be. As I related in *Toughen Up*, I spent a year striving desperately hard to make myself into a concert violinist. Alas, although the will, goal and vision were there, my family insisted I go into the family jewellery business.

Discovering that I could not have a career as a musician was a turning point. It was another hard but easy moment in my life — the decision was hard to take, but eventually it made it easier to move on and get closer to my ultimate goals. And I was left with a deep and abiding appreciation of not just the beauty of music but beauty in general.

A well-balanced life has to include an appreciation of beautiful things. There is so much beauty around us any-way it would be a crime to overlook it.

Beauty is a word like happiness — one we tend to avoid because it sounds a bit vague and soft. There's a suggestion we should be focused on more serious things. But also like happiness, beauty is something we are all seeking in our lives and something I take very seriously.

> **A well-balanced life has to include an appreciation of beautiful things.**

Christine creates beautiful paintings that bring pleasure to many people. She is creating beautiful jewellery designs that will bring pleasure to a very different group of people through our stores around the world.

She and I have made a beautiful home in one of the world's great landscapes. She has created some beautiful art in response to the changes that go on in our surroundings every day through the seasons. Simply being here — having our free time — is a rewarding experience.

My golf course is a work of art in some ways and I have a goal of making it even better by adding contemporary sculptures on each hole. It is set on beautiful undulating land — you constantly come across different views and panoramas that seem to appear out of nowhere. The clubhouse, designed by Patterson Associates, is very organic and has won many awards for its design.

The ability to appreciate beauty is free. And having beautiful things to appreciate keeps you in balance, in harmony with yourself. I have a fascination with listening to CDs of Johann Sebastian Bach, and my favourite CD of solo sonatas for violin features Isabelle Faust.

Bach, probably the most complex composer ever to have written music, is a great inspiration to me. His music can be played in all sorts of different ways. And he never got to a point in his 65 years when he stopped developing because he thought he had achieved everything he needed to. His goal kept extending further ahead and his creativity grew to keep pace with it.

As a result, he is now the composer's composer — the one musicians fall back on because they can always find something new to explore in his work. For a soloist he is a great challenge. He has defeated some of the greatest players of all time.

You could have a lifetime goal of trying to master Bach's playing. That would be a fantastic, rewarding, inexhaustible goal.

They say creative people tend to use the right side of the brain more. I am definitely a right-brain person. I think in pictures. I draw and doodle to help myself think. Often if I can't express something in words straight away, the act of trying to draw it will help me to find the words I need.

I am fortunate to be able to play a musical instrument, but being able to enjoy someone else's playing — or painting, or sculpture or writing — is a great joy also. It enriches our lives and we all have access to it whenever we want.

The only sin in appreciating art is to think you can buy taste. The only rule is to be genuine in what you appreciate. It doesn't matter if the rest of the world thinks it's rubbish, if something makes your heart soar and your soul sing then that is good taste. Also, if the rest of the world praises it but you think it's rubbish, you should be true to your own genuine response.

Personal taste reflects your personality and it's priceless.

7. Easy to be hard

If you're not making some mistakes each year that hurt, you're playing life too safe. Many people misunderstand the concepts of 'easy' and 'hard'. They make so many straightforward things look difficult.

I have referred to this already — when the going is hard it often makes it easier for us to discover a better way forward.

My daughter Emma's progress through the company illustrates this perfectly. She began as a little girl working behind the counter while still at school. Then she did degrees and wanted to go further in the company but others in the management team resisted.

I didn't push it. I didn't say, 'Emma's coming in. I want her doing this.' When you delegate you have to let the people to whom you've given responsibility exercise that responsibility.

Finally she worked her way in and was chosen to help set up our expansion into Canada. And because things were made hard for Emma and she wasn't just bestowed a role as of right, she is one hell of a tough nut. Therefore, a lot of things that would be difficult for other people are relatively easy for her.

Emma is ensconced in her role now. She is deputy chairperson and has her eye on my position. The harder the going is — the more sand you have to shovel to get out of that hole — the easier it is, because you develop an inner strength.

There is another story about Emma that shows this process in a slightly different light because she was the one creating the difficulty for herself.

> **When something is hard it often makes it easier for us to see what we should be doing.**

When she enrolled to do her MBA, she sat in the lecture theatre the first day of the class and felt totally inadequate. She looked around the room and saw people with resumés that included running international divisions of companies. They all seemed very articulate and super confident. She had been working as a Michael Hill store manager.

She sat there trying to avoid the lecturer's eye so she wouldn't be asked to speak. She began to doubt herself. She was no longer sure she had what it took to be successful. But it was the start of learning to step outside of her comfort zone.

Once you identify that feeling, you start to recognise it as a positive one every time it pops up. Something is happening that you are going to learn from, and which will make you stronger.

In that first week Emma discovered you could graduate from that class with distinction. To do this you needed a grade point average of more than 85 per cent. Suddenly, she had a goal.

'If I'm going to dedicate a year of my life to getting an MBA,' she said to herself, 'I may as well get the best MBA I can.'

She set a goal to graduate with distinction and worked with enthusiasm for a full year. Everything came into focus and it was easy to work out what to do because it was all judged by whether or not it aided her goal.

By the time the first exam came around, she was the top student. She got a scholarship for the rest of the MBA and by the end she was the top student for that year. She did the valedictory speech at the closing ceremony and got her MBA with distinction — a very proud moment for us all.

Emma got a fright and turned it to her advantage.

When you are getting started, the small things are harder to obtain. It's harder to make the first $100,000 than the first million — you might need two or three jobs to get your nest egg together. Then things become easier. The 10,000 hard hours are generally followed by many more relatively easier hours.

The tougher the going, the easier it is. Uncle Arthur worked so hard to stop me getting ahead by not selling me his shop that I had a much easier time of it when I set up on my own. If anyone supplied me with stock, he threatened to cancel their accounts so it was hard to get suppliers. If an insurance company was going to cover me, he threatened to cancel his big policy with them.

And it had the reverse effect from what he intended; it just made me more determined. It was wonderful. I owe my uncle an awful lot because had it not been for him and that hardness, if he had sold me the shop or even half the shop, I would probably still only be running one jewellery store in Whangarei, New Zealand.

This has proved to me that being too comfortable is a very uncomfortable way to be.

Before the house fire, things were fine. Christine was earning a good salary. We had two healthy kids, a small boat. We could put a fishing net out and fill it with flounder. I made home brew and sake. We had a great set of friends. We entertained, enjoyed the outdoors and had fun. We had a wonderful life but I always had a nagging feeling there was more.

Then the house fire came and it was easy to see the way ahead. I had a clear realisation: 'There must be more to life than this.' The time I was spending working in my uncle's store wasn't leading me anywhere. But I had an in-depth understanding of the jewellery retail business.

Opening my own store under my name was a revelation — I was totally in charge of my own destiny. It was a momentous occasion in my life. I've never had a moment's doubt or uncertainty in my ability since that day.

Learn from mistakes: frequent encounters with danger are a part of life, making you inwardly strong. I Ching

8. Why life is like a golf course

Designing a golf course is a balancing act. You need it to be challenging enough to keep people interested, but not so challenging that they become infuriated, disheartened and give up. It should inspire them to become more skilled so that they can meet its challenges and improve their handicaps. They like it tough but they want to win.

That's why life is like a golf course.

9. Not the retiring sort

Retirement is not for me.

Many people as they get towards their 50s start to think 'life is probably not going to carry on forever so we will plan our retirement'. They go from doing something to doing nothing.

It is so easy to be conditioned to think like this. The desirability of retirement is implanted in the head at an early stage as a goal to aim for. But if retirement is an end goal, it really means the beginning of the end.

I should know. I tried retirement once.

We moved to the Australian resort of Sanctuary Cove. I had opened lots of shops and thought I didn't need to work any more.

We were surrounded by other people who had done particularly well and decided that the nice option would be to give up their work, buy a lovely home next to the water with a boat at the front and a golf cart at the back. They could take out the boat one day and play golf the next. The weather would always be beautiful. Paradise. What more could you want?

For me it was an amazing experience. I found it completely shallow. I had nothing to look forward to except a vague possibility that my golf handicap could come down (which it never did).

Retirement puts people into a time warp where nothing changes. We lose the initiative to strive for bigger things.

The same can apply to people who don't retire, of course. If they don't develop a 30-year goal, they will still be doing the same thing in 30 years that they are now. I know people who had shops near mine when I first started out. They still have those shops — they are in a time warp — nothing has changed.

For me, the 30-year goal has given me an exciting challenge —

Retirement puts people into a time warp **where nothing changes.**

it keeps me going. Most of us could do so much more than we do. All we have to do is keep going. I found it much harder to stand still than to keep moving.

And the final irony is that the retired people turn in on themselves and become more worried and stressed about things that don't matter because they don't have enough going on in their lives to occupy them. Instead of employing unused brain capacity to do something new, they fill it up with worries about unimportant things.

When they retire, the necktop computer goes into hibernation mode. The memory function starts to pack up. They stop exercising. Their hormone levels drop. Everything seems to slow down because there is no goal in sight and one day is just like another. Look around the supermarket and you can tell who the retired people are — it's not the age on their faces, it's the speed with which they are pushing their trolleys that gives them away. They're not going anywhere.

When people retire they are admitting they have given up enjoying life. The key problem is right there at the end of the word: 'tired'. Please never retire — reset your goals, keep going and enjoy the thrill of the chase.

10. Books that made a difference: 5 & 6

Oh, The Places You'll Go
by Dr Seuss

One of the most profound books I have ever read is about 1000 words long — that's as many as you'll find on about four pages of this book.

It is called *Oh, The Places You'll Go* and the great philosopher who wrote it is Dr Seuss. This so-called children's author wrote more than 60 books, but this one, which manages to convey a whole philosophy of life in such a short space, was the last he finished before he died in 1990. With this book, Dr Seuss proved you don't have to write a lot in order to think bigger.

The book sums up the hopes and fears, challenges, disappointments and victories that come our way as we go through life and concludes that whatever happens to us, life is what we make of it.

The main character, who represents every one of us, sets off on a journey through life, sent on his way with the words: 'Congratulations! Today is your day.' And there you have it — every day is our day. Every day belongs to us, a gift to make as much of as we can.

All is not plain sailing on the journey and the character faces setbacks, complications and hard decisions. But in Seuss's fictional world, as in our own, the worst of all places is where people just sit around waiting and not taking their destiny into their own hands.

I treasure my copy of this book both for its own message and because it reminds me that the really important lessons in life are really very simple.

The Seven Spiritual Laws of Success
by Deepak Chopra

Deepak Chopra's book combines Eastern wisdom with the latest thinking, and provides a guide on how understanding the universal law of nature can lead to personal success. It is a day-to-day reminder of the enjoyment of the simple pleasures that can easily be forgotten in our hectic world. It takes you back to the basics and offers advice on how to lead a balanced yet highly successful life. Chopra quotes from the Hindu teaching, Brihadaranyaka Upanishad: 'You are what your deep driving desire is. As your desire is, so is your will. As your will is, so is your deed. As your deed is, so is your destiny.'

11. Thinking bigger

In 2009 I was named the Ernst & Young New Zealand Entrepreneur of the Year. As a result, Christine and I went to Monte Carlo where the World Entrepreneur of the Year would be chosen from all the national winners. The whole experience was a sensational example of what life is like at a level where everyone has decided to think bigger. There was no one thinking small in this group.

It was a monumentally lavish affair from start to finish. The principality of Monaco is still the A-List jet-set mecca it was in the days of Prince Rainier and Princess Grace. We were put up in one of the finest hotels — I know it was one of the finest because a cup of tea cost double figures.

The final selection was made by a panel of judges who interviewed us all one by one. Even I found this quite intimidating. You had three minutes to tell them about yourself and your achievements and then they asked questions. One judge spent the whole time looking at her notes on the table, which threw me a little. Normally I can engage people quite quickly by telling them stories. But I banished any negative self-talk and kept going. It felt like forever, but eventually she put down her notes and gave me her attention.

The other entrepreneurs included some remarkable people. One had taken Dale Carnegie's advice to dramatise your point to an extreme. He was the English finalist and had an appliance repair service that had done brilliantly. He had brought his company-branded van over and drove it back and forth in front of the hotel. When it came time to do his interview, he appeared in his overalls and carrying a spanner. The panel can't have read Dale Carnegie because he didn't win.

Another person who impressed me greatly was an American internet service provider. He was a beautifully spoken, articulate guy who had done so well he had actually received death threats from his competitors. He had been through a lot and he had a very commanding presence.

The final award ceremony was the most glamorous night imaginable. Even I would have trouble thinking of anything bigger than that.

Christine and I were accompanied by Jon and Caroline Hooper from Ernst & Young in New Zealand. We were picked up from the hotel in a vintage Citroen and taken to the ceremony, which was at another magnificent venue on the waterfront. It had a retractable roof, which was opened up afterwards so you could see an extravagant fireworks display without getting out of your seat. When we arrived, performers from Cirque du Soleil performed amazing acrobatics around us as we walked down the red carpet.

Instead of a bowtie I had a spiral piece of gold jewellery that I wear on special occasions. It's a point of difference. It certainly had an effect that night. When I stepped out of the limousine, all the photographers took one look and suddenly their flashes were going off like crazy. I was stunned. I thought: 'Wow, I must have won this thing.'

I hadn't won. But I didn't feel like a loser — the atmosphere made everyone feel a winner.

While in Monaco, however, I think I had caught a virus of extreme positivity from being surrounded by so many upbeat, successful individuals. These were people who could decide they wanted something and go out and get it.

When you live on a small island such as New Zealand, a true spirit of intense competition rarely develops. I'm glad that we aren't at the point of making death threats to our competitors, but it would be good if we had a steelier edge to more of our business dealings.

It's vital to be quite competitive. It's been a subconscious development, but a lot of what I do outside the jewellery business involves a degree of competition. Golf is a passion and I don't really care whether I win or not when I play, but there will always be a winner in every game. And I've channelled my love of music into the violin competition, which of course is incredibly hard fought and competitive. It's all about the same instinct that drives me in business. It's about being the best.

It would be good if we had a **steelier edge** to more of our business dealings.

Being surrounded in Monaco by people who think bigger reminded me — again — that life is short and there's a hell of a lot more fun to be had than you get by taking the easy option.

You have got to press 'Play' and keep going for it. Then so many avenues open up for you. I came away from Monaco certain that if I wanted something I just needed to be determined and to never stop and just go for it, really. If nothing else, it will keep you young.

Being there confirmed for me that I could be as big as I want to be. There were all these incredibly successful people and I was standing in the same line as them, being judged on the same basis. And both then, and socialising with everyone later, I never once felt inferior or like the lite version of an entrepreneur. Everyone had the same passion as I had.

I took those lessons back to Queenstown in New Zealand and applied myself to my think-bigger goal of expanding into 1000 stores by 2022.

The golf course will continue to be developed. If you own a golf course there is only one goal you can have — to make it the best there is. As with any goal, if you are properly focused on it, the other bits take care of themselves. The good players will turn up. The international golfing world will take more notice. The membership will grow. I am going to keep chipping away at it until we get to that point.

We are sending our young pro and our golf course superintendent to the US Open. They will visit all those great courses and see for themselves. It is the same principle I followed when I made a point of going away for a couple of weeks a year when I was working at the shop in Whangarei. When they get back they will see their old familiar course with fresh eyes and the ideas will start to flow. It is a very good investment.

When you think bigger, big things really do come to you.

It's like what happened, for me, from having a small boat to having a super yacht. I had a nine-footer that grew to an 18-footer in New Zealand. Then when we moved to Australia to grow the business there I acquired a 32-footer. I sold that and bought a 42-footer. Then 56 and now a 112-foot yacht.

Creating a brand

At Michael Hill Jeweller we are in the middle of an exciting plan to develop an exclusive range of Michael Hill products. We have begun with watches, which have been a great success. We're also developing a French perfume, in beautiful bottles that have been designed by my daughter-in-law, Monika. Then there will be Christine's jewellery collection — a branded diamond collection unavailable anywhere other than a Michael Hill Jeweller store. And other products will follow in turn.

Branding gives you a massive point of difference.

But branding is tricky. Michael Hill Jeweller grew with a reputation for affordability and discounting. Now we want to present ourselves in a different light. It is like going back to the girl who rejected you in high school and saying, 'No, I'm not that guy that you didn't want to have anything to do with any more. I've changed, I've changed. I'm quite sophisticated now.'

The advantages of exclusivity are obvious. Say you try on a Prada suit and like it. You might walk away because that suit is pricey and is not and never will be discounted. You look everywhere else but you can't find anything that is cut quite as well, so you buckle and pay the full price for the real thing.

Branding is what makes that happen. Without it, you just end up in price wars with everyone else who is selling apples.

Some major brands have taken 100 years to become established. We are being ambitious in trying to do it in a fraction of the time, but it is a fabulous challenge.

We could do OK simply following what everyone else does. But to become global we need to be unique, find a point of difference and specialise. When we have got a little further in the branding exercise we will be totally unique.

We could have carried on selling the same watches and jewellery or clothes as others, from shops that look the same as theirs. But we noticed that, wherever you go, the jewellers clone themselves to look like the other jewellers. There seems to be comfort in the herd instinct. One of the few jewellers in the US that looks different is Tiffany's.

And if you asked people to name an American jewellery brand off the top of their head, what will their answer be? Of course — Tiffany's.

There is no end to the results we can achieve. You start out trying to close that five per cent gap for the winning edge, then you get down to four per cent . . . Finally it's a quarter of a per cent gap. Then you've done it, so you recalibrate, think of a bigger goal and start over to close the gap between you and the next competitor who is five per cent ahead of you.

In a lot of companies, you will notice after one or two generations, there is a tipping point where the great established names start to vanish because they do not evolve. The vision of the founder got them established and kept them going but that founder was almost certainly a dictator. He never passed responsibility to anyone; life became easy for his family with their trust funds, so they never developed a vision of their own. When the founder goes, things can go downhill very quickly. They could have been reinvented and grown even greater.

We are not going to fall into this trap. We are 30 years old and outside that cycle. This founder has delegated his vision to other people and they will keep the business growing because I have encouraged them to think bigger.

You have to make adjustments and constantly alter your plans. We've got the right model now. We have a centralised base in Brisbane, Australia, with a warehouse and distribution for every store around the group from one location.

I think it is important we retain the family feel to the culture. To achieve our goal we need several hundred new managers as well as other staff. To find them, we could have put an advertisement in the situations vacant pages of the newspaper. Instead we put on a show.

The idea came from my New Zealand general manager, Greg Smith. On a cold June night in Auckland I found myself on stage presenting an evening at the Skycity Grand Hotel. It was part motivational seminar, part self-help lecture and quite a lot recruitment drive. We sold tickets and the proceeds went to the Cure Kids charity.

Around a thousand people turned up. I sat and signed books before the show started. I got the impression a lot of people had come because they were very hungry for inspiration. They were not happy with their lot. Many looked stuck in routines and jobs they didn't like. They wanted to think bigger and just needed a few basics to get them started.

There were a lot of couples who came and lots of groups of friends who maybe thought they could find an adventure to go on together. They heard from some of the brightest stars among our team, including Emma. Without exception, everyone told a story of how working for us had let them achieve things they had never dreamed possible. We had several people make enquiries afterwards and have taken some on.

One young man was typical of the sort of people who are attracted to work with us. He was part-way through a degree and not enjoying it. His father had offered to buy him a franchise of his choice when he was ready, but halfway through the evening apparently, they looked at each other with the same thought: Why buy a franchise when he could be as successful working with us. We told him to take a couple of weeks to think about giving up his degree. He did and he is joining us very soon.

He is a very talented young man and his future looks very rosy. It would have been worth doing the whole exercise just to have someone of his ability join us.

For the people who do join us, we will set a 30-year goal with them and share the dream of where the company is going. They can go from salesperson to trainee manager. At that point they may decide they would like to be a manager. Then in five years they could become a district manager for New Zealand or Australia. If they did that they might end up, after 10,000 hours, as the general manager for another country. The sky is the limit!

We have people who have followed paths like this. This is a company that promises significant career goals. We also try very hard to advance the people who are already with us before looking outside. It would be wrong to encourage people to think bigger if they weren't going to be able to translate that into action.

For those who come along with us, there is no limit to what they can do if they let go of their negativity and

think bigger.

keep going!

12. Books that made a difference: 7

Toughen Up by Michael Hill

I was thrilled with the response to my previous book. Here are extracts from just a few of the emails and letters I received from readers.

> Before I had a chance to purchase myself a copy, my father turned up handing me a copy after reading it himself (he purchased one for each of us three boys).
>
> Once I started reading it I also insisted my best friend read it. Unbeknown to us at the time, he was made redundant after 15 years at his employment shortly after. Somewhat shocked, he sat down the next day, saw an advert for a great job in the paper, applied for it, and started reading your book, that day, writing down his goals and visualising his new position. You got it — he now has the job, about a month after being terminated.

> I have just finished reading your book, which has inspired me to get back up and start fighting again in a business sense. The message the book gave me was to never give up and if you work extremely hard life will turn around. Once again, thank you.

> Thank you, your book is the kick in the bum that I needed.

> Your story and philosophies are so relevant and have hit home in an amazing way. Only halfway through the book yesterday I took a few hours off from meetings, etc. and put pen to paper on ideas for the business goals and strategies. Then with a real focus from reading your book and using visualisation on what I want the business to look like, in two hours I had five short- to medium-term goals and a 10-year goal drafted. More importantly I now have a real drive to not only

achieve these goals but smash them. Now these weren't all new ideas or goals but in reading your book it has inspired and encouraged me to rethink them and more importantly put them to paper and always have in front of me as a living reference point. I went out and purchased a plain paper ideas book for my own reference point that would always be with me and I can add all my ideas at any time, and more importantly go back through in the future to make sure I am still on track. I already have six pages of ideas and goals noted down.

My business is currently experiencing some of the toughest challenges it ever has and I want you to know that reading your book has given me the courage to stand up and use these times to make a real difference. There are many parallels in the book that I relate to and your story is so 'real' that this is the ONLY book of this type that I have read that has armed me with the tools to turn our business back into a GREAT business. I want to thank you personally for putting pen to paper.

Coda for people with no time to read

Think Bigger
the condensed version

Choose a goal

↓

Believe in it

↓

Take care of yourself

↓

Think bigger

↓

Repeat

So this is the end — or is it the beginning? Whatever it is, it is up to YOU. To get the most out of this book I suggest you do read it, or skim-read it again and highlight with a coloured marker things that take your attention.

The ideas in this book of course, are only my own personal ideas on the way I conduct my life. Possibly they are not for you, and I understand this, but one thing I guarantee will bring you exceptional results is to goal set. Plan your future and join the half a per cent who do plan and achieve miracles with less effort.

Also, please watch your health and listen to your body. It will tell you how it feels, so please listen.

And finally, listen to your inner instructions and enjoy living in the present. Stop worrying, start living with your new exciting challenge and leave a mark on this planet as someone who has achieved greatness.

I guess from now on it's over to you. Good luck and best wishes,

Michael Hill.

www.michaelhill.com

Further reading

Ageless by Suzanne Somers. Crown Publications, Random House USA, 2006

Escape to the Pole by Kevin Biggar. Random House New Zealand Ltd, 2010

Food Rules by Michael Pollan. Penguin Books, 2010

Hitting the Zone: Golf at the Top with Steve Williams, by Steve Williams and Hugh De Lacy. HarperCollins Publishers (New Zealand), 2004

How to Win Friends and Influence People by Dale Carnegie. Vermilion, 2006

Oh, The Places You'll Go by Dr Seuss. HarperCollins Publishers, 2003

Out of Darkness by Zoltan Torey. Pan Macmillan, 2004

Outliers: The Story of Success by Malcolm Gladwell. Penguin Books Ltd, 2008

The Lazy Way to Success: How to Do Nothing and Accomplish Everything by Fred Gratzon. Soma Press, 2003

The Power Program by Dr Michael Colgan. www.colganinstitute.com

The Seven Spiritual Laws of Success by Deepak Chopra. Bantam Press, 1996

The Three-Minute Meditator (5th edition) by David Harp and Nina Smiley. Mind's I Press, 2008

Toughen Up by Michael Hill. Random House New Zealand Ltd, 2009

Save the Brain by Dr Michael Colgan. www.colganinstitute.com